Ar cue

Contents

Finding the rabbit

On Monday we went for a walk with our mum.

We saw something moving in the grass.
It was a baby rabbit and it was hurt.

Mum said we should put the rabbit in a box and take it to the animal rescue centre.

A lady called Julie runs the animal rescue centre. “What have you got in that box?” she said.

At the animal rescue centre

Julie took the rabbit out of the box.
"It's hurt," she said. "We should take it to the vet's."

Julie telephoned the vet's. The vet said he could see us at three o'clock.

Julie looked after the rabbit. First she gave it some milk.

Then she got the rabbit some food and a basket to take it to the vet's.

Going to the vet's

We put the basket in the car and went to the vet's.

When we got there we felt a bit scared.
“Don’t worry,” Julie said. “The vet will
make the rabbit better.”

The vet looked at the rabbit all over.
“It’s a female rabbit,” he said. “And she has been hurt by a dog.”

The vet put some cream on the rabbit and gave the rest to Julie. “Put this on the rabbit every day,” he said.

A new home

We took the rabbit back to the animal rescue centre and put her in a hutch.

This is the rabbit's new home and Julie lets us see her every day!

Index

TIMELINE HISTORY

GAMES

From Dice to Gaming

Liz Miles

Raintree

www.raintreepublishers.co.uk
Visit our website to find out more information about Raintree books.

To order:
Phone 0845 6044371
Fax +44 (0) 1865 312263
Email myorders@raintreepublishers.co.uk

Customers from outside the UK please telephone +44 1865 312262

Raintree is an imprint of Capstone Global Library Limited, a company incorporated in England and Wales having its registered office at 7 Pilgrim Street, London, EC4V 6LB – Registered company number: 6695582

First published in hardback in 2011
Paperback edition first published in 2012

Edited by Louise Galpine and Diyan Leake
Designed by Richard Parker
Original illustrations © Capstone Global Library Ltd 2011
Illustrated by Jeff Edwards (map, p. 5) and Darren Lingard (card suits, p. 11)
Picture research by Hannah Taylor
Originated by Dot Gradations Ltd
Printed and bound in China by CTPS

ISBN 978 0 431 02556 8 (hardback)
14 13 12 11 10
10 9 8 7 6 5 4 3 2 1

ISBN 978 0 431 02564 3 (paperback)
15 14 13 12 11
10 9 8 7 6 5 4 3 2 1

British Library Cataloguing in Publication Data
Miles, Liz. – Games : from dice to gaming. – (Timeline history)
795-dc22
A full catalogue record for this book is available from the British Library.

Acknowledgements
We would like to thank the following for permission to reproduce photographs: akg-images pp. **6** (Erich Lessing), **13** top (Alameda Films/Real Madrid TV/Transglobe Pictures/ Wanda Films/Album), **14** bottom; Alamy Images pp. **9** top (© David Hancock), **10** bottom (© Interfoto), **11** (© The London Art Archive), **12** (© Jake Lyell), **22** top (©Interfoto), **23** top (© Jon Bower Thailand), **24** bottom (© Jenny Matthews), **26** (© StockImages), **27** (© Network Photographers); Corbis pp. **7** bottom (Jack Fields), **13** bottom (Francis G. Mayer), **15** bottom (Oliver Weiken), **16** bottom (National Archives/ Science Faction), **20** top (BBC), **20** bottom (Hulton-Deutsch Collection), **22** bottom (Klaus Hackenberg), **25** (Philippe Lissac); Getty Images pp. **4** top (AFP/John D. McHugh), **9** bottom (Michael Springer), **21** (AFP/John D. McHugh), **23** bottom (Time & Life Pictures/Ralph Morse), **24** top (Bill Greenblatt); istockphoto p. **17** top (© Vladimir Ovchinnikov); Photolibrary pp. **8** (Peter Holmes), **19** (Jose Fuste Raga); Rex Features pp. **4** bottom (Etienne Ansotte), **18** bottom (Nils Jorgensen); Rijksmuseum p. **14** top; The Art Archive pp. **7** top (Kanellopoulos Museum Athens/Dagli Orti), **16** top (Musée des Arts Africains et Oceaniens/Dagli Orti), TopFoto p. **15** top); © V&A Images/Victoria and Albert Museum, London pp. **10** top, **18** top.

Cover photograph of a trade show for computer and video games reproduced with permission of Alamy Images (© Jochen Tack).

We would like to thank Bill Marriott for his invaluable help in the preparation of this book.

Contents

Historical time is divided into two major periods. BC is short for "before Christ" – that is, the time before the Christian religion began. This is the time up to the year 1 BC. AD is short for "Anno Domini". This is Latin for "in the year of our Lord", meaning the time from the year 1 BC to the present. For example, when the calendar says the year is AD 1000, it is 1000 years after the year 1 BC. The abbreviation c. stands for *circa*, which is Latin for "around".

Any words appearing in the text in bold, **like this**, are explained in the glossary.

People of all ages like to play games. We play games for fun and to compete: everyone likes to win! Games can teach, too. They help us practise skills, such as how to add up, spell, or follow rules. Physical games – for example, hopscotch – teach body skills such as jumping and throwing. Dolls and toy animals teach children to **role-play** and care for things.

Children often have a favourite teddy bear. This bear was made in 1904.

Popular toys and games have changed over time. The timeline in this book will show you how toys have developed. New materials and new **manufacturing** processes bring new toy inventions to the shops. Different toys can be popular in different countries. People's toys and games are influenced by their **culture**, taste, and wealth.

Computer games are quite a new invention. This Nintendo DS game **console** was available worldwide in 2009.

Timelines

The information in this book is on a timeline. A timeline shows you events in the order they happened in history. The big timeline in the middle of each page gives you details of a certain time in history (see below).

Some dates are exact. For example, the first talking doll was invented in the year 1823. Others are more general because people may not have kept written records or the event happened over a period of time. The smaller timeline at the bottom of each page shows you how the page you are reading fits into history as a whole. You will read about games from all around the world. Each entry on the main timeline is in a different colour. This colour shows you which continent the information is about. The map below shows you how this colour coding works. Pale green indicates events that took place on more than one continent or worldwide.

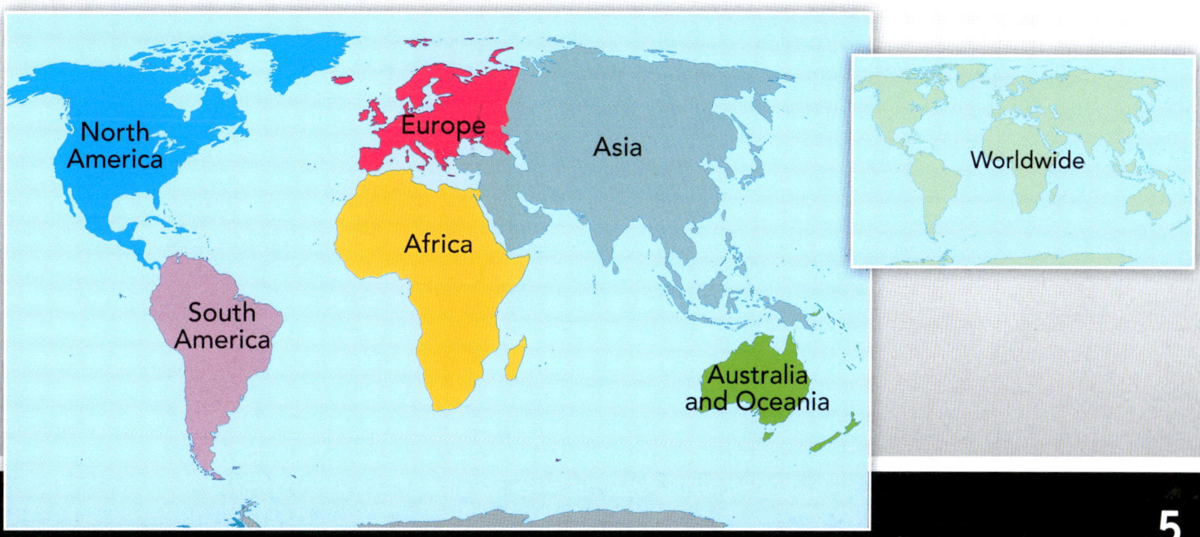

Ancient beginnings

Some of our toys and games were played thousands of years ago. They were handmade from simple materials such as wood, stone, **terracotta**, and metal.

*c.*3000 BC

A board game similar to **draughts** was played in Mesopotamia (an area we now call Iraq). This stone board, 14 pieces, and 3 dice were found buried in a royal tomb.

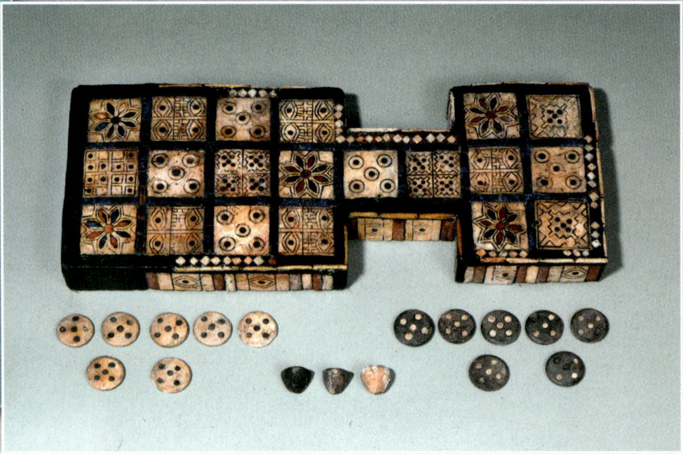

*c.*3000–1800 BC

Ancient Egyptians played with stone marbles.

*c.*2500 BC

The ancient Indus Valley **civilizations** left behind toys such as clay animals on wheels.

*c.*500 BC

Ancient Greek texts describe yo-yos made from metal, wood, and painted terracotta. This Greek warrior toy is made from terracotta.

1000 BC 500 BC 1 BC

*c.*206–230 BC CHINESE KITES

The oldest known kites come from the time of the Han **dynasty** in China. Kites were used to measure distances in the Chinese emperor's palace. There are ancient stories of kites carrying men into the sky. Chinese dragon-shaped kites are still flown for good luck.

Toys as tools

When **archaeologists** find old toy-like objects, they cannot be sure if they were made just for play. Some old "toys" were made for other purposes.

AD 286–476

In ancient Rome, boys had small bows and arrows. They practised shooting arrows as training to be good soldiers. Boys played a game similar to today's hopscotch, too, perhaps to improve their hand and foot skills.

AD 250 | AD 300 | AD 350 | AD 400 | AD 450

c. AD 300

Adults often played games just for fun. The Indian game of pachisi was played by emperors and princes. It was a board game like the ludo that is played today (right). Small shells were thrown instead of dice.

AD 325–925

The Mayan **civilization** made "worry dolls". They were lucky charms, not toys. Today people tell their worries to these dolls. They hope the dolls will take the worries away.

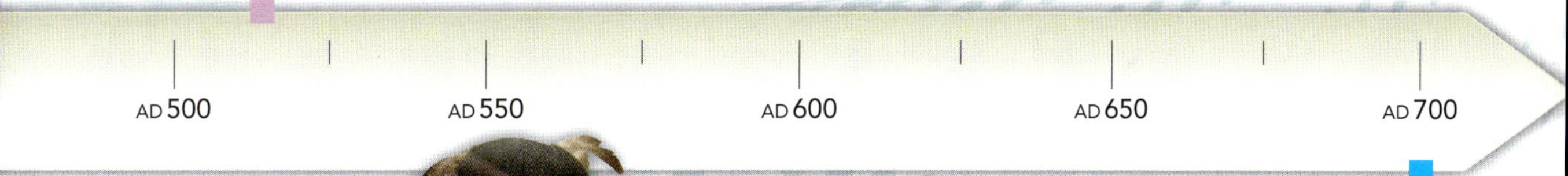

c. AD 700 Kachina dolls

Native American Hopi people carved kachina dolls to look like the gods from their myths (stories of ancient gods and heroes). Parents used kachina dolls to teach the stories to their children.

Remember the rules!

Games with complicated rules were played all around the world. For example, players had to remember how different game pieces moved and what cards to play.

AD 600

People in India played a game called chaturanga. Over time it became the game we know as chess. The pieces were characters such as king, queen, horses, elephants, chariots, and foot soldiers.

AD 600 AD 700 AD 800 AD 900

AD 1100

Chess was very popular in the Middle Ages. These chess pieces from the 1100s are carved out of walrus tusk. They were found on the Isle of Lewis in Scotland.

c. AD 1280 Alfonso's book

King Alfonso X of Spain put together the first book of games played in Europe (*Libro de Juegos*). It describes the rules of games. Many of the games in Alfonso's book came from overseas, such as nine men morris from Egypt and backgammon and chess from India, shown here.

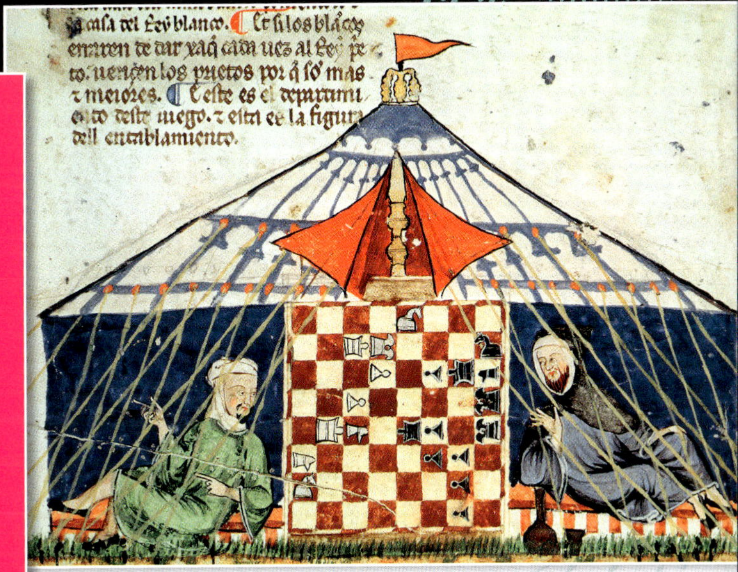

AD 1300

By this time, Egyptians were playing with decks of cards similar to today's. There were 52 cards and 4 or 5 suits (sets of pictures). The suits included coins, swords, staffs, and cups.

AD 1300

The Maori of New Zealand played cat's cradle, making patterns by twisting a single piece of string between their hands.

Balls, bones, and stones

Ready-made games such as chess were only for the very wealthy. Ordinary people still made their own toys or played games that needed nothing at all except for the players.

1450s

African tribes played a game which is still played today. It has a board of small holes carved into planks of wood or dug in the ground. The two players try to capture each other's pieces, which are stones or dried seeds or beans. The game has different names in different part of Africa. One of the names is hus.

1440 1460 1480 1500

1500s

Shove-groat was a popular game in **taverns** in Shakespeare's England. A groat was a coin. Players had to shove coins along a table to reach special marks. It is still played today and is called shove-ha'penny.

1500s

When Spanish explorers reached America they saw people playing with a rubber ball for the first time. The Mayan **civilizations** used sap from trees to make the first balls that bounced.

1520 1540 1560

1560 Bladder balls

This painting from 1560 shows that most children did not need much to have fun. They played leapfrog or used wooden sticks and hoops. Balls in Europe were made from a range of things, from animal **bladders** to skulls. The bladders were blown up. The game of **knucklebones** used animal bones!

Who played with this?

Many toys and games were enjoyed by a certain group of people. For example, expensive dolls' houses were a favourite toy among rich European women.

1600s

The first dolls' houses were made for adults, not children. Wealthy women in the 1600s paid craftsmen to make them.

1600 1635 1670

1613

Dutch **settlers** were the first to play skipping games in North America. But only men played them. People worried that girls might hurt themselves!

1700s

A board game called mancala has been played for thousands of years. By the 1700s, it was played (mainly by adults) throughout Africa and Asia.

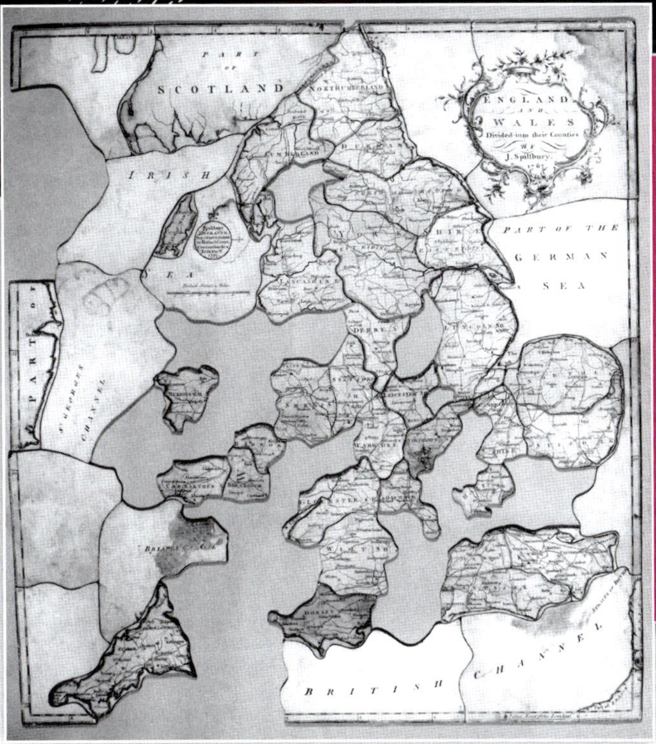

1767 Toys to teach

The English **philosopher** John Locke (1632–1704) believed toys could be used as a teaching aid. He made some letter blocks to teach boys the alphabet. One of the first jigsaw puzzles (left) was made in 1767 for schoolchildren. It was of a map used to teach geography. Jigsaws became toys in the 1820s.

1705 1740 1775

1700s

At first, **pedlars** in China used a diabolo to attract people to see their wares. In Europe, diabolo became a game for the upper classes. It is still used today in China for exercise to keep fit.

Toy revolution

During the **Industrial Revolution**, factories began **mass-producing** toys in England, then Europe and North America. Mass-production made toys cheaper. There were also new materials and inventions, such as talking dolls.

1800s

Changes in **manufacturing** did not reach Africa so quickly. Most toys were still homemade. This doll from Cameroon was made in the 1800s from wood, beads, and shells.

1800 1820 1840

1823 Crawling and talking dolls

The first talking doll was made by a German inventor. The doll said, "Ma-ma" and "Pa-pa". Lifting an arm worked bellows (air-filled bags) inside, which made the sounds. Inventors started to make moving dolls, too. Pins and cogs, like those inside a clock, made dolls walk and crawl. The doll in the picture was made in the 1870s.

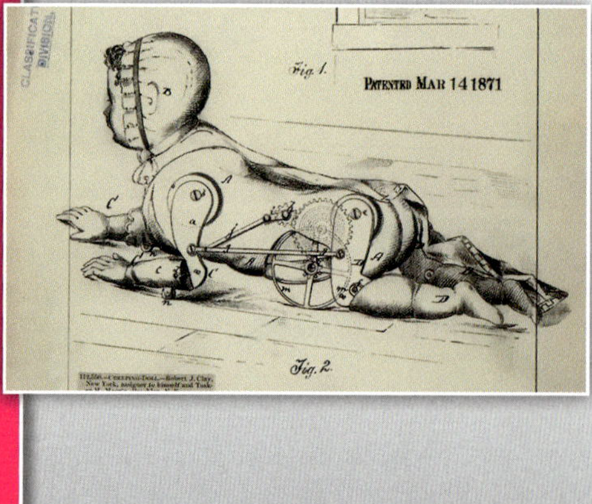

1890s

Toys like these matryoshka dolls were still handmade in Russia. Each wooden doll can be pulled apart to reveal a smaller one inside.

1860 | 1880 | 1900

1892

The ancient Indian game of snakes and ladders became popular in England. It was used to teach children how to behave, as counters went up a ladder when they came to a "good" square and down a snake when they came to a "bad" one.

Big names

The toy industry grew, and companies such as Steiff, Parker Brothers, and John Waddington made lots of money.

1900

Countries in Asia still made carefully crafted **one-off** toys, such as this pull-along elephant made in India.

1915

There were no toy shops in **remote** parts of Canada. Instead, Inuit people who lived there carved toys out of animal bone.

1900 1905 1910 1915 1920 1925

1902

The German company Steiff made their first toy bear. Every Steiff toy has a little button in its ear to prove it is made by Steiff. People in the United States named toy bears after their president, "Teddy" (short for Theodore) Roosevelt.

1920s

The first **pachinko** machine was made in Japan. It became such a popular game that rows of adults now **gamble** on them in places called pachinko parlours.

1949

The Danish company Lego sold the first famous fit-together plastic bricks. Six Lego bricks can fit together in at least 102,981,500 different ways.

1930 1935 1940 1945 1950

1935 Clever inventions

Parker Brothers brought out Monopoly. The "money-making" board game helped Americans to forget their poverty in the **Great Depression**. In the 1940s a game called Candy Land was invented. It was popular as a way of "giving children sweets" without the bad effects of eating real sweets.

1948

The word game Scrabble went on sale. More than 100 million sets have been sold worldwide.

I saw it on TV!

In the 1950s some of the first television programmes were made for children. The viewers wanted games linked to the programmes. Advertisements encouraged people to buy games.

1950

A popular television programme called *Andy Pandy* was first shown in the UK. Toy versions of the characters went on sale.

1950 1952 1954 1956

1950s

Toys such as this Australian koala were often covered in real animal fur. Soon factory-made fibres such as **nylon** and polyester replaced animal fur. It was more **hygienic**, cheaper, and ensured no animal was killed to make the toy.

1959 Plastic bodies

In the United States, the first fashion doll went on sale. She was called Barbie after the maker's daughter. The **moulded plastic** method of making toys meant that thousands of identical dolls could be made cheaply.

1958 1960 1962 1964

Mid-1960s

A New Zealand company started to make metal car models. It was part of a worldwide craze. More families owned cars, so more children wanted toy cars to play with.

1964

The first G.I. Joe "action figure" was made for boys in the United States. In the United Kingdom, it was called Action Man. Some people thought that **military** toys encouraged children to be violent.

Crazes

New toys came and went, depending on the latest craze. Just before Christmas in 1984 all the cloth dolls called Cabbage Patch Kids were sold out, but in 1986 everyone wanted a Transformer.

1970s COMPUTER FIRSTS

Nintendo, a company in Japan, released the first colour TV **video game**. Players used paddles to hit a ball. The first popular game was Pong, made by Atari in 1972. It was a tennis-style game played on a TV screen (right). The computer craze grew in 1989 when Nintendo released **Game Boy**.

1970 1971 1972 1973 1974 1975

1975

The puzzle called Rubik's Cube was named after its inventor, a Hungarian professor named Ernö Rubik. The puzzle can be moved into 43,252,003,274,489,856,000 different arrangements, but only one is right!

1980s

In **remote** rural places, many children did not (and still do not) have modern toys. This Indonesian child is playing on stilts made from local plants.

1976 1977 1978 1979 1980

1977

After the movie *Star Wars* came out, *Star Wars* **merchandise** sold well. More money was made from *Star Wars* books and toys than from the film itself.

Collect the set!

International advertising makes toys popular worldwide. Clever **marketing**, such as making sure items are rare, encourages people to want whole series of toys or cards all the more.

1990s

Nine types of Beanie Babies were launched. Later, more of these bean-bag animals were made. Only a few were made of some types, to keep them rare.

1990 1992 1994 1996 1998 2000

1997

The Pokémon Card Trading Game was released, based on a **video game** from Japan. It was invented by Satoshi Tajiri, whose idea for the "pocket monster" cards and pictures came from his love of collecting bugs as a boy.

2006 Here Wii go!

New video game **consoles** produced realistic moving pictures. They were Microsoft's Xbox 360, Sony's PlayStation 3, and Nintendo's Wii. Wii (pronounced *wee*) lets you play a sport such as tennis in your lounge! The console picks up the way you move a special racket or **remote control**. Wii Sports is marketed as a way of keeping fit.

2005

Kite fighting was banned in Pakistan. For fighting, kites are attached to wire covered in powdered glass. The wire is used to cut away opponents' kites. The sharp wires had injured people.

Good and bad

Many parents worry that today's popular computer games keep children indoors too much and stop them from playing together. Even board games can now be played by a child alone, using a computer.

Present
This is a game of chess played on a computer.

People also worry that cheap plastic toys use up too many resources, and the world's resources are running out.

Traditional toys

The answer to these worries might be to play more traditional games, such as hopscotch and skipping. They are healthier and use fewer resources. But many children will always want the latest toy or best computer **console**. And computer games can stimulate the mind and help with **dexterity**.

Present

Many children are too poor to buy toys or computer games. They make their own games. These children in Brazil have made a **draughts** set using bottle tops.

Safety

Toy safety is important, too. If the paint used on toys contains lead, this can cause poisoning that may harm a child's brain. Toys may have small parts that can come loose and cause problems if children swallow them. Many countries have passed laws to make toys safe.

Key dates

c.3000–1800 BC
Ancient Egyptians play with stone marbles.

c.206–230 BC
People in China use kites to measure distances.

c. AD 300
People in India play pachisi, which is a game like ludo.

AD 600
People in India play a game called chaturanga, which becomes the game we know as chess.

1280
King Alfonso X of Spain puts together the first book of games in Europe.

1300
The Maori of New Zealand play cat's cradle.

1450s
African tribes play hus. The two players try to capture each other's pieces, which are stones or dried seeds or beans.

1500s
The Mayan **civilizations** use sap from rubber trees to make the first balls that bounce.

1600s
The first dolls' houses are made.

1760s
The first jigsaw puzzles are made for schoolchildren.

1823
The first talking doll is made by a German inventor.

1892
The ancient Indian game of snakes and ladders becomes popular in England.

1948
The word game Scrabble goes on sale.

1959
The Barbie doll goes on sale.

1975
The Rubik's Cube is invented. The puzzle can be moved into 43,252,003,274,489,856,000 different arrangements.

2006
New **video game consoles** produce realistic moving pictures. These are Microsoft's Xbox 360, Sony's PlayStation 3, and Nintendo's Wii.

Glossary

archaeologist person who studies what has been left behind from the past. Future archaeologists might dig up one of your old toys.

bladder a bag-like organ in the body. Animal bladders can be blown up like a balloon.

civilization particular society or culture at a particular period of time

console small box or panel of controls

culture customs and beliefs that a group of people has

dexterity skill with your hands

draughts a game for two players, played on a chequered board

dynasty ruling family

gamble make a bet that something will happen in the hope of making money

Game Boy small, battery-powered video game system

Great Depression period in the 1930s when money lost its value and many people were poor

hygienic completely clean and won't make people ill

Industrial Revolution time of sweeping change when masses of people moved from farming into industry

knucklebones game in which you throw and catch small bones or other objects with one hand

manufacture make something, usually in a factory

marketing making people aware of things to buy

mass-produce make things in large quantities

merchandise goods linked to a film or book

military to do with the armed forces

moulded plastic plastic that is formed by pouring it into shapes, called moulds

nylon a strong fabric made from chemicals

one-off item that is unlike any other item

pachinko a game in which a ball whizzes round into a hole

pedlar person who travels around selling things

philosopher someone who tries to work out the meaning of life

remote far away from other people and difficult to reach

remote control box that controls a device from a distance

role-play act as if you are someone else

settler person who goes to live in a different land

tavern drinking house. Today we call taverns pubs or bars.

terracotta clay that has been heated to make pottery

video game electronic or computerized game

Index

Find out more

Books

***Ancient Olympic Games* (The Olympics series)**, Haydn Middleton (Heinemann Library, 2008)

***Cricket* (Know Your Sport series)**, Chris Oxlade (Franklin Watts, 2006)

Sport Files series (Raintree, 2008)

Welcome to the Ancient Olympics!, Jane Bingham (Heinemann Library, 2007)

Would You Believe ... the Losers Were Killed in Mayan Football?: and Other Perilous Pastimes, Richard Platt (Oxford University Press, 2007)

Websites

Learn lots of different ways to play hopscotch:
home.howstuffworks.com/hopscotch-games.htm

Find out about record-holders in a range of sports and games on the Guinness World Records website:
www.guinnessworldrecords.com/records/sports_and_games

More about the famous bear company, Steiff:
www.steiffteddybears.co.uk/steiff_interest.asp

Places to visit

Pollock's Toy Museum
1 Scala Street
London W1T 2HN
Tel: 020 7636 3452

V&A Museum of Childhood
Cambridge Heath Road
London E2 9PA
Tel: 020 8983 5200
http://www.vam.ac.uk

The Fight of my Life...my Purpose and the Pain

By Leanne Burke

Purpose Publishing
Derby United Kingdom
ISBN: 978-09570550-1-8

Printed in the United Kingdom

Contents

Foreword

Leanne is a valued member of All Nations for Christ and it is a pleasure and a privilege to write this forward on her behalf.
As soon as Leanne gave me the manuscript, I could not wait to start reading.
I began on a Friday night and I thought I would just read a few pages before going to bed. However, I was gripped by the story line and could not put the book down. I continued reading into the very early hours of Saturday morning.
I began reading again on Saturday afternoon and did not stop until I had completely finished the book.
At a young age, Leanne went through an incredible journey. The book outlines her pains and struggles and shows how God showed up for her with His grace and favour in the midst of her troubles.
As you read this book, I believe you will be strengthened and encouraged and reminded that no matter what you go through there is always hope. I pray that God will lay someone on your heart who is going though a difficult time, please be a blessing to them and buy them a copy of this book, it will be a great inspiration to them.
God bless you, Leanne, this is your first book, it is tremendous and I believe you will be the author of many more books.

Apostle Patrick Dawkins
Senior Minister of All Nations for Christ

Acknowledgements

This has been a long journey, and I have so many people to thank. If I don't mention you, please charge it to my head and not to my heart; I love you all dearly.

First and foremost, I have to honour God. Without Him, none of this would be possible. He is the author and finisher of my faith. He has brought me this far, and I know there is a long way to go, but by His strength I will make it.

To my parents…if you didn't keep going with me regardless of the messes I made, where would I be? I am thankful to have parents like you who ensured I always had the best of everything. The values you instilled in me even when I wanted to resist them have contributed to the 'new' me and I am thankful for you each and every day.

To Apostle Patrick Dawkins, you are so blessed. Thank you for being so transparent in your living. What God has planned and ordained for you, eyes have not seen and ears have not heard. It is a privilege and an honour to be involved and to be a member of your ministry.

To Pastor Sandra Dawkins my First Lady. I love you dearly and I am so grateful to have you in my life. Over the years which are now many you have always been such an inspiration and role model to me and I thank God for you each and everyday.

Minister Sonia Dawkins, He is still in control. Thank you for all your support and love; you are truly blessings in my life. Love you.

To Bishop Walter J. Smith, (my dad) you are truly the vessel. I praise and thank God for you continuously. Thank you for releasing the things of God into my life. Love you always.

Minister Frances Cooper, love your spirit, your heart, and again your transparency. I thank you for your continued support and encouragement. Thank you for imparting words of wisdom into my life. I will never forget the day you told me that I was an eagle and that I had to fly with the eagles. I love you always.

To Sandra Baugh. Love you more than words could say, you have been a great support to me. More than you know.
To my auntie Edna, love you very much and thank you for being you.
To Miss Carmen Cooper Rose as I like to call her, words could never describe so I won't attempt to articulate how glad I am to know you- but you know! Love ya!

The three way crew Lori and Samantha, I got crazy love for you both, it has been a great journey together thus far and I can't wait to see what the future holds for each and everyone of us.

And to my dear friend Jassette, my dear friend because you tell me the truth always, when I am right I am right but when I am wrong I am wrong. Your friendship is valued more than you know and I love ya, xxx

To my beautiful godchildren. You are all truly blessings from Heaven and I take it as an honour to have you. Mac-Kye, Rebekah, Nyarah and Reuben; Aunite Lee-Lee loves you endlessly. You are all the future and this is your world, so make the best of it and be who you want to be.

To all my true friends and family here and gone, it has been a long journey, sometimes up and sometimes down. But at the end of the day, this is me and you dealt with me as me. You didn't judge me; you believed in me and saw where I could be, as opposed to where I was. I love you and pray God's blessings over your lives.

Finally, I send this book to every person that has ever been through something, to the broken-hearted, to the people that have come to the end of themselves and cannot see the light at the end of the tunnel. To you all I say NEVER give up! You can make it, because hey look at me…This is It!

All my love,

Lee-lee (Leanne)

Introduction

(Note: Names in this book have been changed to protect the identity of real-life characters.)

I am not writing an account of everything that happened in my life, over the course of this book I will brush over a lot of things en-route to deeper revelations, which are inserted to encourage, inspire, and motivate my mass audience. I had to overcome a lot to reach this point in my life. It wasn't easy, but it was worth it. I fell down, but I was able to get back up again through His grace and continuous mercy. His faithfulness to me is beyond measure, as is His love.
You may ask what warrants a twenty-four-year-old young lady (I still refer to myself as a girl!) to write a book about her life story. What kind of life could she have had that would be able to be put in print and impact lives all over the world? The answer to that is ... you won't know until you read my story. I can testify to a life, which was leading me down, down, down. I can testify to the miry clay because I was in it and sinking, sinking, sinking. I have had the abusive relationships, the divorce, done the crimes, and nearly died so many times. I have been to 'hell' and back, but I am still standing, and I am here to tell you about it. I am here to share a piece of my life with you, so that in my mess you may receive a message and a sense of hope.

Don't give up, because a quitter never wins and a winner never quits. Be a winner. Don't give up the fight, because when you least expect it, your opponent will feel the twitch, and that last blow will knock them out for the count. You are a winner!

1
World at My Feet

I was born into a loving, warm family, but it was not always like this. Before I was born, my family consisted of my mum and dad; three sisters and one brother.

My dad was a builder, and he had formed his own business in this field, whereas my mother was trained as a psychiatric nurse, but at the time chose to practise as a general nurse. They enjoyed family life and the fact they were able to embark on having their own careers, as coming from the West Indies was really hard for black people during the eighties.

As the children got older, it became more and more apparent that mum and dad did not want any more children; therefore, they made a conclusive decision for my mum to have an operation to prevent her from being able to have any more children. My mum was enjoying working life and, I suppose, didn't want any more breaks in her career.

She had the operation and it was a success, as far as she and the doctors knew. Let me just mention at this point that when God wants to bless you and perform a miracle in your life, it does not matter what man-made barriers are in the way; nothing can counteract His blessings. She went back to work, and the family all got on with their lives. She was working part-time night shifts to ensure she was always at home to attend to the children when they came from school. The two youngest children were at private school and doing well, and Claudette by this time had moved out and was working two jobs to keep herself.

It was a good few years later when my mum was at work and realised she had been feeling strange for a few weeks. She called her friend, who was also a nurse, and at forty-three years old, my mum asked her if she thought that she could be going through menopause. She was adamant that this would be the case because of all the symptoms she was experiencing. The suggestion was made by the friend that maybe she was pregnant, to which my mum assured her friend that it would not be possible.

After visiting the doctor's office a few days later, my parents found out that they were expecting another child. The shock alone overwhelmed them, as they couldn't understand how this was possible.

They were thrown into confusion as they tried to process this information in their minds. The strangeness of how this came about was a miracle in itself. It emerged that my mum was seven months pregnant with me when she finally found out I was there; she did not have an idea in all that time that anything was wrong. My mum was an experienced mother with four other children, let alone the fact that she was a nurse and, therefore, well-learned when it came to signs and symptoms of being pregnant. She didn't even experience morning sickness. This is where you have to stand back and admire God's handiwork, concealed and growing in my mother's womb for seven months until I was revealed.

Whilst we are on the subject matter, I just want to let you know that when you have an extensive operation as my mum had, it makes it impossible for you to ever have children again, as all connections are severed. So somehow these connections grew back to their maturity to enable me to be conceived. It's hard to get your head around it, but again I say look at God's handiwork.

My mum could not work it out either, and it was because of this that she and my dad decided to take a trip to London to see a specialist in regards to compensation. It was explained to them that, even though the procedure has an overall high success rate, the percentage was only 99 percent and, unfortunately, they had fallen into the 1 percent.

My mum was broken, as she was at the pinnacle of her career and now she was to bring forth this child that was not planned. Whether the child was wanted or not was not an option at seven months.

What was once a semi-perfect family turned into a war zone type of family, because of something that normally would bring joy. Where was the happiness and the rejoicing? Initially, there was sadness and despair, despair of the unknown. At my mother's age in those days, it was not common to carry a child, as there could be side effects and the child could emerge deformed.

Being a man of faith, my father decided to commit the situation into the hands of God so that God's will would be done. He knew that this was a miracle from God, and he knew everything would work out. My father also found himself confiding in a family friend, Ruth, who

also presented the situation to the Lord in prayer.
One day out of the blue, my mother had a conference with my father and confirmed that she was not happy about it at first, but she had decided to keep the child.

My parents shared the news with their other children, and they were so happy to know they were to have a new baby brother or sister. Days, weeks, and months passed, and as the family went through the motions of everyday life and preparing for the new arrival, the time was drawing nearer and nearer. The day finally arrived, and my mum was rushed into hospital in labour. You can imagine all the bits in between on the way to a healthy, bouncing baby girl being born on November 16, 1983. That bouncing baby girl was me, and this is my story.

Leanne. What's in a name? When I was born, my mum said she didn't have a name for me, but she clearly heard God telling her to call me Leanne. She didn't know what it meant, but upon researching all of my names, I found that Leanne means to be gracious and full of grace. Jane means God is gracious, and Deborah means a bee or swarm of bees. My full name is Leanne Jane Deborah Burke.

Days mounted upon days, and the presence of the new arrival quickly sunk in and was noticeable. My siblings were so con- sumed with curiosity, as they played with me, looked after me, and loved on me. They seemed to be in awe of this creation called Leanne and were excited and ready at every chance to show her off and fight over who would look after her. My second older sister, Claudette, took to me like a charm. She spoiled me at every chance and professed nothing was too good for little baby "Lee-lee." She spent as much time with me as she could and always took me out and bought me the best toys and clothes. There was an immediate change in the atmosphere in the home. There was a certain peace that fell over the family, and bonding was allowed to take place. Finally, everyone was smil- ing and was filled with joy, all because of me and my birth. Friends and family were ecstatic at the knowledge of my birth, and they revelled at the chance to have me to themselves. I used to wish I could go back to those days, when I had no worries or cares, just a baby and looked after, incapable of getting in trou- ble. But I soon had to wake up out of that crazy dream.

Looking at my mum's old passport, I realised the first time I was taken on a plane was at nine months old. It was our 1984 family reunion in New York. Obviously, I didn't remember anything about it, but the fact that I have beautiful photos to help me create images of times gone by is crystal.

By age two, I started nursery and was also sent to summer school. By this time, my mum was back to work full time; therefore, as well as being with my brothers and sisters, I spent a lot of time with my dad. The next few years, I was travelling everywhere he went, as he had to look after me. I enjoyed it because I was able to meet new people. Eventually, my brother and sisters left home and our town of Derby, so it was just me. No more playing or the sense of being loved. I was left alone by the time I turned three years old, no one to talk to, just me. I believe this is why I ended up being shy all of my life. Growing up alone meant that I would talk to myself for company. At our church, I was the only child for a while, and then when there were kids, they were many years younger than I was.

I started private primary school at the age of five. Even now, whilst I am writing this, I vaguely remember activities and actions that used to be carried out. Again, as a pupil at private school, I was sheltered—the real world didn't really exist. All I knew was school,

home, and church. Oh, and I can't forget the private classical piano lessons that I used to have every Tuesday at five o'clock p.m.
I used to enjoy playing the piano most of the times, but I must admit I loathed the fact that I had to do royal graded examinations. But I passed, so after the nerves I revelled with joy for each accomplishment every time.

My dad was a preacher, so, as previously mentioned, I used to travel all over the country with him, which was great because of the vast amount of people I used to meet. Even though I was shy, the people always made an effort to talk to me and be nice to me, which was great because they spoiled me—and every child likes to be spoiled.

I excelled in school to the point where, I remember, my head teacher had to skip me two grades. I was put in a class with older kids, and it was great. I felt important, because it was noticed that I was what they called brainy. To me, brainy did not mean anything; I was just happy to be moving on up in the world. A few years later, the creative side of me kicked in, and I was inspired to start a school magazine. It had never been done before, and it didn't look like it ever would happen unless I did it. So I approached my head mistress with a letter I had written explaining my ideas and thoughts. Wow, when she called me into her office, fear gripped me, because she wasn't that nice of a person. I may have gone into a cold sweat (I don't really remember), but I went. When I left that office, I was happy internally and externally. She said yes; she was willing to support my idea. When I was ten, I got my first Compaq Presario PC, so I had been teaching myself to use it to design and produce my school work and projects. I was so glad that I got a team of friends together, and we organised ourselves and worked out what we were going to produce. The magazine was a success. The kids in the school loved it. Finally, I was doing something that I enjoyed and made me happy. I should have noticed from then that I enjoyed being creative and loved spending time perfecting my handwork for public consumption. Maybe if I had noticed from then, I could have had my passion tamed, and I would not be such a workaholic now … but I'm not complaining.

At the age of thirteen, it was decided that the secondary school would close, and only the primary part of the school would remain open. I was so comfortable there that I became scared of having to move on. We looked around for a few schools, which I hated, and my mum even took me to Ockbrook boarding school, which I made up in my mind I would do anything not to go to. I explained to my mum that I wanted a change; maybe we should try a state school. It was the worst thing I could have done. So I was enrolled in Murray Park School, starting 3 November 1997. I was still shy and didn't communicate much.

From what I saw around me, my head starting to pulsate at a fast pace. Remember, I had been fully sheltered for thirteen years of my life, and then I was thrown in the deep end. This was totally my fault, as I did not want to obey my parents. I heard words and conversations and witnessed behaviours that I never had before in the entirety of my life, I mean come on, I wasn't used to swearing, fighting or seeing people get beaten up and left bleeding before; it was all new to me. I was in an alien environment and hated it. I wanted out, but it was too late. I was surrounded by what I thought were strange people, and they probably though I was strange also. I remember I did not speak; I kept to myself. If I was spoken to, I would respond. Otherwise, you would not hear a word from me. I felt so scared and disrupted within me. This is why I started forging letters from my mum excusing me from school and classes I didn't like. I used to just walk out of school if I wasn't happy, hoping that it would not be noticed. I would go to town and sit in the library and do my work. Anything was bet- ter than being in that darn school. I remember one year we had reports, and my overall attendance was 46 percent. Can you imagine? I had to hide the report from my mum. Years preceding it declined even more. By this stage, I was not going to the library anymore, but travelling between twenty to fifty miles outside of Derby to Nottingham and Birmingham.

Even though I was hardly at school, I never fell behind with my work. I was always ahead of time and always had to put on the façade to my parents that everything was okay with me, even though it wasn't. Being like an only child growing up, I developed a strategy of wanting to please people all the time. I had within me the desire for people to always speak well of me. I didn't want to give anyone anything but good to say about me. Even when I was doing the worst thing ever, if I saw someone I knew or who knew my parents, I would instantly change. I knew that I couldn't afford to accrue a bad name; maybe I should have remembered that in those years to come, when trouble was going to come knocking at my door as a consequence.

At the age of fifteen, I remember I was at the bus stop and met a man. Well, rather, he ran into me—literally. We got talking and, next thing I knew, Clive had my number. Then we started talking often. I remember the first time I went to see him was in Birmingham, because he had gotten in trouble in Derby and had to leave swiftly. I started going to Birmingham often to see him, as we formed a relationship. I started doing things and exploring areas that I knew nothing about. Yet again my world was chang- ing. I was entering territories I never dreamed about, getting involved and associating with subjects from the drug and crime underworld. Remember, I came from a sheltered life, so this relationship thing was strange to me. I started lying to my parents and telling them that I was going on school trips after school. I would go to the train station and get the train to Birmingham nearly every day to see this man that I suddenly thought I was in love with. It was so overwhelming that I got to the point where I confided in my sister —yes, the one who was so close to me as a child—and she failed me. Because I was shy, I was not the type of person to talk to my mum and dad about myself, my life, and my problems. So I thought I could trust her. How wrong I was! She told my parents that I was sexually active and that I could be pregnant. Can you imagine, being fifteen and pregnant? My home turned into a war zone. My mother was so distressed and upset; my father did not say much, but you could tell he was upset. I couldn't get through my head why Claudette did it. I trusted her, and she broke that trust I gave her.

I was due to go on holiday, and I remember my mum telling me that I couldn't go anymore and that she was ashamed of me. I was adamant in tell- ing her I was not pregnant, but she didn't believe me. I had bought an early pregnancy test and, a while later, found out I wasn't pregnant. I was so over the moon! My family was scarred for a while, but it was an opportunity for the healing process with my parents to begin and be completed.

Maybe I should have mentioned that Clive was old enough to be my dad. I was fifteen and he was forty-two, but I did not know much different. I liked him. Looking back now, I don't know why, if I did it over again, that I wouldn't. But then maybe I would, because I had to go through that experience to be here now. It made me a much stronger person. He was from Jamaica, and he was a drug dealer. Yes, that is what I said. He was the first drug dealer I had ever met, so I didn't know what he meant when he said that I was the opposite of streetwise. I was clever academically, even though I was truanting school, but when it came to things that happened in the ghettos, I knew nothing.

So our relationship kind of tapered off when my mum was informed, because I was forbidden to go back to Birmingham. I had to tell a lot of lies to be able to sneak over there and go, but my mum was on to me like a hawk eating a worm. Eventually, Clive went back to Jamaica, as his time was up and he didn't want to overstay (so he could come back again). We said our good-byes, and he said he would be back for me soon. "Soon" turned into I'm still waiting! After my time with him, my life declined. I went from man to man to man, one-night stands and degrading five-minute stands. Relationships didn't last longer than one month. I didn't even know what I was looking for; friends that I had acquired along the way were doing it, so I did it too.

It was exam time at school, and I was trying to complete coursework and prep work in eleven subjects. As I said, academically I was mint, but the amount of time I spent on the road instead of in the classroom was appalling. You wouldn't think I would be doing my work, but I was.

After exams I left school and closed a chapter of my life to start another. I remember the August when we had to come back to get our results—I was so scared. At one point, I was reading my grades and checking to see if it was really my name on the scores or someone else's. I passed with high grades in my eleven subjects. That wasn't me; even at that age and the condition I was in, I recognised that it had to be God. If it had been me, I would have failed.

I was finally able to make that crucial decision: work or higher education. Well, I did both. I got my first part-time job at Somerfield

Superstores, and then I applied to go to sixth form college at the Millennium Centre in Derby to study English, Information and Communication Technology (ICT), and Media Studies at advanced level.

2
Rebellious Nature

Sometimes it seems hard to break certain habits and cycles. At the time, I did not understand anything about this and the impact that cycles would have on me, but I was pursuing what I thought I wanted in life. I say 'what I thought' because we all come to the river, as it were, in life, where we have to decide whether to cross or stay for a while until we feel we are able to cross, or we come to the road where we have to choose which path to take. There I was, confused, feeling used, maybe depressed—definitely oppressed— and not wanting to let other people or my parents down. Obviously, in that situation you are going to attempt to do what they want. So that's why I chose higher education. But it was not what I wanted. I started and all was well, until the feelings of not wanting to be there, which I had felt at my secondary school, set in. One day off turned into one week, into one month, and so on. I was leaving my house each day, acting as if I was going to college, but I was knocking around with friends, bad company, and then-some.

I made some really good friends this time round, but even they began to realise that I was never in college and would go as far as making jokes about it when I did turn up. I wanted to be there, but every day I had to wake up to face another day; I couldn't do it. I felt so down in the gutters that to be in a class- room was wounding. It was strange that this was the case, as I had no problems with walking up and down the streets, idling with my friends' day in and day out.

It must have been January 2002 when I was at the petrol station with my best friend at the time. She was having "choccie" cravings, as she was about eight months pregnant, and a car with two guys inside drove up. If my memory serves me well, one of the guys got out, passed his number through the glass, and told the attendant to give it to me. In my mind I was thinking, 'What is this crazy geezer doing? I don't want his number, and he needs to move from me with that.' As I said, that was in my mind, but my friend took his number. I was going to throw it away, and she said to keep it. How random was that? I mean it was strange, right? So I kept this number, and all that was on my mind was what had happened and the fact that I had this number. I promised myself I would not ring it, so I folded it up into a tiny piece and stuffed it in the back of my purse. If that was now, I would have thrown it away, because when you make up your mind about something, you need to get rid of anything that will tempt you to go against your final decision.

I remember going to church on that Sunday, and I did not hear anything that happened there that day. All that was on my mind was the fact that I had this number and I didn't want it, but out of curiosity, I was going to ring it. Have you ever heard that curiosity killed the cat? Well, it did!

I came in from church and ran up to my bedroom, flung my things down, and jumped on my bed. I lay there for a while, staring at the ceiling. I was really acting like a girl in love, bearing in mind, I had nothing but a glimpse of this man who communicated his number to me in this odd way. I had a conversation with myself in my mind, and I nearly talked myself out of calling him until I heard something say, 'well, what harm would it do?' A double-minded man is unstable, and I was setting myself up for a fall with what I was about to do, but I didn't know that at the time. I had no experience in life. I was young and experimenting with life to learn things the hard way. I know you are sitting there and asking, "Well, what happened? Cut to the chase!" Okay, so I called him, and he didn't answer. I felt relieved that he didn't, as I didn't know what I would have said to him in the event that he did answer. Then the unthinkable happened: he called me back! I answered the phone casually, with a small, sweet, shy voice. "Hello? Who's this?" as if I didn't know. He replied and started a conversation. The only thing he really wanted to know is if I had a man and if we could be friends. Obviously, I said 'no' to the first one, bearing in mind that Clive had left the country, and yes to the second question, because I didn't mind making new friends. Junior and I started talking more regularly on the phone and seeing each other every day until I couldn't wait to sleep and wake up so I could see him again. I was still barely going to college, but not concentrating, always wanting to be with this man whom I hardly knew but who seemed to have a great impact on me.

I started going to his house every day and spending all my time with him, until I dropped out of college completely. My parents didn't notice, as I was still putting on a show and making them believe I was going. I remember I was still doing my work at home, because I had exams coming up and I wanted to sit them.

I wasn't the kind of person to question someone about his life, as I didn't want to impose and seem like I was being nosey. I found that I hardly knew much about Junior, yet he questioned me about every aspect of my life and expected an answer. So I decided to ask a few questions about him, to which he gave me an answer. I have always been able to decipher when people are telling me lies, and I always had the feeling that there were things he wasn't telling me, but I did not have any proof. So I had to accept it until I knew differently. He appeared and acted so nicely, and he always treated me well. He bought me whatever I wanted when I wanted it, and never had a complaint. He was so encouraging and appeared to want the best for me in all areas of my life. He even helped me to revise and prepare for my A-level exams, which were a success, as I passed all three of them with reasonably good grades. This drew me closer to Junior, as he seemed like an ideal figure to be in my life and share my life with. I wasn't in love with him yet, but I was on the way by all means. He made me what I thought was happy and, at the time, that was all that I needed.

Apart from Clive, this was my first serious relationship. I think I would have done anything to keep the feeling that I had. The more we spent time together, the deeper my feelings got for him, which is why, when he sat me down one day and told me that he loved me but he had to pay someone to marry him so he could get his stay in England, I felt like my heart was breaking. I wouldn't marry him because I knew my mum wouldn't allow it, and remember what people thought of me was always an issue. But I was heartbroken. I remember Junior saying to me that we would still be together, but he would just be married to someone else.

Being brought up in the church, I knew right from wrong, even though sometimes I did wrong. I knew I couldn't marry him. On the other hand, my mum had been proclaiming that she was having dreams about me and that I was hiding things and doing wrong. Obviously, I was denying these things, and, on the inside I felt like I was dying because I was lying to my mum. But how could I admit that everything she was dreaming about was true? Once again, I was at that crossroad. Which way would I go, left or right? I loved this man, I lied to my parents, and he needed to get his stay. What would I do? Where would I go? After contemplating it for about a month or so, I decided that I couldn't allow anyone else to marry him while we were still together. I don't know what was ruling my head and my heart; I was making these decisions without counsel, without really thinking them through, and not realising the consequences. When I told him what I had decided, he was over the moon. So three months into our relationship, I was eighteen at the time and he was thirty-one, and we began to find out how to go about getting married.

I had made this commitment to him, but I felt so empty inside. I was getting married, and I was scared to tell my parents and friends. My friends were already worried about the fact that I had become like a recluse. I did not interact with them on a level that they were accustomed to, and they hated it and hated him. To be honest, they were right. One thing about Dutchpot (Dutchpot and Dutch were nicknames I used to call Junior) was that he did not like my friends. He preferred for me to be with him or at home, but not with my friends. It was to a point where I totally cut off everybody; I didn't speak with them anymore. The only friend I kept was my best friend, who had recently had a baby, and he

did not even like her. How could I tell her I was getting married? I did not want anyone to know, because I lived in such a small town, where everyone knew everyone's business and loved to chat too.
Over the years, I realised that there was nothing that I could do without my parents knowing, because people would always find a way to tell them. So, can you understand why I always had to be good in the eyes of my parents and other people?

About one month into the relationship, I began to see a side of Junior that I was scared of. He liked to beat up anybody who got in his way or offended him. A few times, I remember he had to hide from the police because he stabbed somebody, and he beat someone else and left him for dead. I could not get my head around the fact that this is the man I thought I loved and was going to marry. Don't get me wrong, he had never raised his hand to me at this point. But looking back, if that was now, I would know it was a set up for disaster. With his temper, he could be capable of anything.

After the beating of someone with a crowbar and nearly kill- ing them, Junior moved out of Normanton to Sinfin, where I semi moved in with him. I say 'semi', as I lived at home and was still hiding my relationship from my parents, even though they were not stupid and knew everything. We moved to Sinfin and spent a number of weeks decorating and setting up the house so it was comfortable. Again we spent time together constantly, to a point where I was there for two weeks. I didn't contact my family to speak to them, but I always used to call when I knew no one would be there. I would leave messages on the answer phone so they knew I was alive. Two weeks passed, and I was scared to go home. I was scared of the wrath of my parents. My best friend rang me one day and said my mum had been to their house looking for me, and she said she was going to call the police because I was missing. Can you imagine, Leanne a missing person? I have to laugh now; it sounds funny. That was what prompted me to go home and show my face. When I got there, you could imagine the stress I was then under. "Where have you been? What have you been up to? How could you do this?" and the list goes on and on and on. I felt like rubbish. Yet again I had let my parents down, all en route to disaster. I was causing them pain and heartache, which they really did not need at their age. By this time, they were about sixty-two years old. I felt so sorry, but, on the other hand, I was so attached to this new person in my life that I felt like I needed him. He had become my rock. Without him, I felt empty and alone. I decided that I was not going to pull that stunt again, but I couldn't stop seeing him. So then I began sneaking out late at night and staying over, then coming in every morning around five o'clock a.m. I used to think I was getting around my parents. I used to think I could pull the wool over their eyes, but it was not happening. Even when they didn't say anything, they knew.

In the midst of all this, I felt like I needed to get away. So I decided to apply to go to University. Dutch was having problems with people and his anger, which was far from in control, and needed a change also. Therefore, I applied to go to Nottingham, which was about twenty-five miles away from my home to study for a high national diploma (HND) in computing. I was scared to leave my mum. While growing up, I never wanted to be too far from her, so I thought it was far enough but just about close enough at the same time. It was far enough to be able to live comfortably with Junior and in peace, not having to hide at every turn.

I got accepted to the institute in Nottingham, which then prompted me to look for somewhere to live. I was used to good living from when I was young and was not prepared to live just anywhere. My new home had to be to a certain standard. I found a perfect brand new flat in Radford, and I snapped it up instantly. Finally, I felt like my life was on track. I started to make my plans, and I informed Junior. He became happy at the thought that maybe he could start a new life somewhere else.

In the meantime, he began to tell me things about his life, slowly but surely, as he began to trust me more. I am the kind of person who, if you tell me something, I never forget. So I know if you are lying, if you come with a different story. Anyway, he told me that he had two daughters in Jamaica and that he was no longer with his babies' mother. But he wanted his children and their mother to come over for the summer. Heck, I loved him. I didn't care. I was in agreement with everything. It shows that, in theory, things sometimes sound better than in reality. It is only when the actual happens, and you feel the reaction of it, that it hits home that you should have thought about it first. How could I have told him that I didn't want him to see his kids? I couldn't do that. It wasn't even the kids that bothered me. It was the mother that came with the kids.

Time went on, and they came for their two-month holiday. Yes, I said two months. It felt like my world had ended. I did not spend as much time with him as I used to. In fact, I hardly saw him at all, as he had to spend time with them and her. I felt like my heart was breaking. He would occasionally come and see me at night-time for short periods of time, but it wasn't the same. In my mind, all I was thinking of was him with her and them doing things they were not supposed to. I felt like I was going mad. I started to hear voices, and it was not nice. I had no friends, because I had to cut them all of for him. He was in total control of my life. Then all of a sudden, I was free to do what I wanted whilst he was not watching, but I couldn't because I had nothing to do and with no one. He set me up really well. So he knew I could be trusted, because I had no one.

Although all these feelings were killing me, I still loved him. He was still my heartbeat, my friend, and my partner. Toward the end of August, I started to pack up, as I was moving to Nottingham to start school in the beginning of October. My dad said I was going to get away and do my own thing. He just didn't know how right he was. That was the exact reason; otherwise, I wouldn't bother to move. If I had moved out of home but stayed in Derby, people would still see me and report back on me. I had to be out of the way, so I could just live my life how I wanted.

Junior and I eventually moved to Nottingham. I remember the night so clearly like it was yesterday. At one point, they were unloading the van and put the sofa on the pavement while they came in with some other things. Within seconds, there were people running to pick up the sofa and carry it away! I couldn't believe it. All I heard was "teef teef" (for those of you not familiar with patois, he was saying thief) as Junior ran down the street after them. It was so funny. I think they must have been scared of Junior, so they dropped the sofa on the pavement and ran off.

We settled in and were happy. One thing about Junior is that he liked to play a lot. He was always messing around, and, I must admit, I am ticklish and then-some. I used to get mad at him because he always went too far and played too much. But we were happy. I know, right, the first guy I got involved with was in his forties, and now again a guy way older than me. Some kind of pattern was developing here.

What was I looking for—a relationship or a parental figure in my life? I think I wanted to be in a relationship but needed someone who was able to be in con- stant control. Again this was attributed to the fact that I lived a sheltered life and was just trying to work things out for myself at the time. So I needed someone to give me freedom, but to also set the boundaries.

I began University College and I was really into it. I was enjoy-ing going. I had a bit of a slow start, as usual, because I was shy. I didn't talk much, so other students found they had to work really hard to get through to me. But in the end, the hard work paid off. I then had to look for a part-time job to cover expenses, as it wasn't easy being in education and having no income. I was spending faster than it was coming in, and I had become some- what addicted to the nicer side of life. I had credit cards and cheque books, and I wasn't messing around; if I could spend it, I did. I took out credit accounts with stores like Dixons and Currys and was literally living a life of riley. Not one thought of how I would pay for anything, just spending. I looked around for a job and got a position at a Department store in Nottingham. Outfit was a department store kind of like Macy's or Debenhams, and I was a Sales Assistant there. Again I enjoyed it to begin with, but I got bored easily, which was not good. I started to feel depressed whenever I was away from Junior for too long. I used to wake up in the mornings and the thought of having to leave him at home and knowing that I wouldn't be with him used to make me physi- cally sick. I felt like I couldn't survive without him. I felt like my heart would stop beating if he was not by my side. I don't know how he felt, but I knew how I did.

College was going well, and I was ahead with my work as usual. My grades were good, but I was also getting bored in this area of my life.

It was something that I was not realising at the time: how I couldn't stick with anything, how I would lose interest after a period of time. This pointed to all directions where I was unstable. I wasn't able to continue with anything I started, because I felt voids in my life, which I did not know how to fill. Somewhere along the line, I gave up on church, feeling they were too hypocritical for me. I believed 100 percent in God. I loved Him with all my heart, but I was confused. I couldn't understand His supposedly chosen people who were to worship Him. They did not live the talk or walk the talk. They would say one thing and do the opposite. I could not be in that predicament, as it confused me more. So I gave up. I pursued a life of looking for happiness, which I thought I had found with Junior. It was okay for a while; things couldn't have been better. But if it is forbidden, it will never last.

Slowly but surely, I started to fall away from college and stopped going. In the meantime, I started to occupy my time with wedding preparations. We set the date for 19 November 2002, and time was approaching swiftly. I designed my dress and got it made. Back in those days, I used to love designing clothes and making them. I always dreamed of becoming a fashion designer, but that dream fizzled out when one day when a lady at my church told me maybe it would not be a good idea, as I couldn't design what the "World" wanted. Basically, I could not design what the world, on a whole, would be interested in, because it would be a sin according to her that is not according to God, or the Bible. Apparently it would be too risqué, on the other hand I saw it as her not wanting me to follow my dreams. Maybe she was scared I was actually going to amount to some- thing good in life. Can you imagine? For all of my younger life, when I had a thought of what I wanted to do when I grew up, I would be set back by someone relating the bad reasons why I couldn't do that. My choices were always made for me. Anyway, enough with remembering the hurt and pain of my past… .

We organised the wedding and everything was set. In my mind, I was battling with whether to tell my parents or not. I was scared. I wrote letters to my mum and destroyed them out of fear. I wanted her to know, but couldn't pluck up the courage to tell her. It was already going around Derby that I was married, and my parents had heard. Of course, they asked me and I denied it. I wasn't actually lying, as I was not married yet, but the guilt continued to consume me.

When Junior lived in Derby, he made money the only way he knew how. It was the worse way, and many could call him an involuntary murderer, but it was his thing. Hustling on the streets of Derby day in and day out was something he kept away from me, as he realised I was oblivious to this kind of living. I suppose it was my naivety that protected me at the time. He came in one day and decided that he couldn't stay any longer. He felt low because I was paying for everything.

The rent, the shopping, the bills—everything was me—and he felt like he was worthless. He wanted to move back to Derby so he could continue to do his thing. So he put this to me, and I didn't want him to leave. I didn't want to move back either. It was so hard to decide. I needed to be with him, so I decided I would commute from Derby to Nottingham every day to work and we would move back. We decided a date and arranged everything. Then we were back in Derby. I did not tell my parents; they thought I was still living in Nottingham for at least three years after I left. I was doing well with my job, but boredom continued to set in even worse, as I had to travel twenty miles by train each day to get there and back. I slowly began to slack and miss work, but I couldn't tell Junior that. He always encouraged me to go to College and work. If he knew I wasn't going, he would have been mad. So I kept it from him. I eventually found that I was in the same position with him as I was with my parents: lying to him about what I was doing and where I was going, just to keep the peace.

3
Secrets and Lies

The wedding day was not far away and Junior wanted his friend Garfield to come over from Jamaica for the wedding. He asked me to write an invitation letter for him. I mean, back in those days, it was easy for people to get into the country. All they needed was this letter and they were in. So, if my memory serves me right, we picked up Garfield a week before the wedding. He seemed like a nice person, but looks can be deceiving. Junior used to smoke a lot of cannabis, and I knew the effects of this drug would take its toll on him one day. He had been doing it from the age of thirteen, and he was hooked. Every time you would see him, he would have a spliff, even in bed.

At this point, we had three people living in our two-bedroom house. Can you imagine? I was sharing a house with two men, and one of them were not the tidiest of beings. I felt like I had no privacy or space. I thought that it would be for a short time, only to have that taken away from me when I overheard Garfield in a conversation a few days after he came that he was planning on staying over here. I didn't understand why. What would he do? Sell drugs too? Get arrested and deported? I mean, that's what they all did, wasn't it? It's like they couldn't do an honest day's work. It was get rich quick or not at all.

Back in those days, I was young and quite naive. I was not used to this kind of living. I didn't know about gangs, guns, and war, but I was learning—and very quickly. One day, I stumbled into my bedroom to find Junior sitting in the corner on the floor cleaning out a gun. I instantly went into auto pilot and went on like I wasn't shocked and scared, but deep down inside I was shaking and scared. It was a gun and bullets, in my house, for what? Where did it come from, and what was he going to do with it? I had never seen a gun in real life, let alone be up close and personal to one.

I remember that I used to hear deals going on in my living room in regards to weapons and bulletproof vests. A bulletproof vest? What for? Why did I have to be in the midst of this? Because of disobedience and wrong decisions that I had made. I always say, if I knew then what I know now, would I have made different decisions to cap the pain and heartache that I went through? We will never know.

Bullet-proof vests, I knew, were used in gang warfare and the gun culture world. But what I couldn't understand was why they were in my space. One thing I began to realise was the fact that I seemed to have seeped into this world, which was totally con- troversial to what I was used to and to how I was brought up. I mean, I grew up with a Christian upbringing and lifestyle that was immediately opposed to the dark side in every aspect. It was like the scene out of Grease where

Sandra is good, but to make her man happy and to fit in, during the next scene she's wearing black leather and has a cigarette in her mouth. You could even go as far as to say it was good versus evil. This is where I was. This is where I had reached, and I was still sinking. These things were happening to me, and I allowed the devil to take control, because I pushed God out. He no longer existed to me. I had allowed my boyfriend to stop me from going to church but that was an excuse for me to really get out because I couldn't survive the nature of the people.

As much as I wanted to be in church, the passion was killed within me, killed because of the people that surrounded me. Killed because of their attitudes and how they were towards me. If I was to start talking about the experiences I had with church folk, you would be surprised, people who over spiritual- ise everything to do with God and make lives miserable. People who make God look like the nasty kid in the playground and he is not. Don't get me wrong I love them dearly and I am not trying to get at them, I've passed that, I've forgiven all that, I've been delivered from all that; but memories still remain. It came to the point where I didn't pray anymore. I did nothing that reflected that I was ever a Christian or that I was even brought up in that kind of environment.

We used to go to London a lot. In fact, it was almost every Sunday. We would drive down the M1; well, I would drive, even though I didn't have my license yet. Looking back, I think now that anything could have happened to me back then. I could have gotten arrested or gotten into serious trouble for driving illegally and not having insurance. I know if my parents had known, they would have been so distressed. (Mum and Dad, I know that you know now, and I'm sorry).

Some chances that I used to take back in those days I would

never take now. I just didn't care; it was almost as if I didn't have a conscience. I would try nearly anything once; there was no caution in the bad choices that I made. Excuse me while I go off on a tangent sometimes. As I reminisce on events to contribute to this account of my life, I seem to end up going deeper into consequences. It's a pity I did not think about them before. But one thing with Junior was that it seemed as though he loved his family which in England consisted of his mum, sister, and cous- ins so much, even though sometimes they disagreed.

The love and respect was from both sides. They seemed to like me too, but in those days I was shy. I did not do much talking, not more than the usual hello, bye, and yes or no. I really have to laugh—can't help it—because people who know me now say that I am anything but shy, which is true. I am so lively and outgoing nowadays that shy is not an option. All I can do is attribute it to the love of God… . There I go again on a tangent!

About two weeks after we moved back to Derby, our wed-ding day arrived. It was a Tuesday, and the weather did not want to smile with me. It was the first day that I saw Junior's real colours. He shouted at me on the morning before the ceremony. I couldn't believe it. He shouted at me, for nothing, and whatever he was going through was not even my fault. I felt so hurt and dismayed. How could he? All that was going through my mind was, Is this really him? Had he been pretending all these months to be a nice person? What had I got myself into? My head was in a mess. I couldn't back out though; it had to go ahead. I was too scared about the consequences if I had changed my mind. It went ahead, and I spent the whole ceremony distressed and upset at how he had spoken to me in the morning.

We were married, and it was the majority of his family that came from London. I had one friend whom I trusted not to tell anyone. I was so down. No family, no friends to share my day, just me and strangers. Can you imagine? My wedding cost three thousand pounds, and we had a small reception afterwards. I spent the day and the night asking myself what I had done, won- dering if it was a dream and if I was going to wake up soon, but it wasn't happening.

The reception was okay; everyone enjoyed it aside from me. I sat there miserable, contending with the voices in my head. I heard this was for life, and I would be stuck with a man that I no longer thought I loved. Can you imagine what that is like? Unless you have been in this situation, you would not know. A lot can happen in ten minutes. I can start the ten minutes off in my right mind and in my right name, and by the end of the ten minutes, I can be married, have a new name, and a new destiny that is not for my good.

On the same night, I asked Junior a few questions. They were the questions that I had asked him before, but inside I needed to know that he wasn't lying to me. I hoped that he would give me the same answer as he did all those months ago. So I asked him when his birthday was, and he told me a different date than when he initially told me; furthermore, it was a different date than what was on our marriage certificate. I asked him various other questions, and he answered me differently. I think he realised I was on to him when he told me to stop being farce and trying to work things out in my head. I couldn't sleep that night. I knew there was something wrong. I knew he was lying to me that night, but how many more things did he lie about? What were lies and what was truth?

My mind was in turmoil. What had I done? What had I brought on myself? Can you imagine knowing someone who is supposed to be close to you has lied to you? You can't trust anything they say, because it could be lies. But you love him, because even thought he has lied, some part of you wants to overlook the fact. Some part of you says that person can do no wrong. But who was I to judge him? I was no better. I was lying to my friends and family about my relationship and about what I had done.

I continued to lie to my friends and family, feeling guilty day in and day out, getting deeper and deeper in depression and oppression, which was attributed to this mistake I had made.

Life at home was mediocre in the beginning. We had known each other for eleven months, and throughout, Junior had been consistent in mood and behaviour—until the wedding day. He apologised and looked like he was genuinely trying to make an effort and make our relationship work. But this fantasy was often short-lived when his temper got the better of him, and I felt the impact of his stress and tension somewhere on my body. On a number of occasions, it came to the point where I used to pack up my clothes and things and load them into a cab. Then I would go around to my mum's house. I'm sure she used to wonder what was going on, but as she didn't even know I lived with a man, I couldn't exactly venture into detail why I was there and the beating I had just experienced. Junior used to call me after a few hours, and he would ask me where I was and when I would be coming home. The conversation was typical. It would always continue with me saying that I wasn't coming back, because I couldn't take the beatings anymore and I didn't want to live like that. It would then continue with him telling me how much he loved me, that he didn't mean to do it, and that he would never do it again. Eventually, before the end of the conversation, he would manipulate me into thinking it was all my fault why he had a violent temper and my fault why he hit me. And the unbelievable thing is that I actually agreed with him! I agreed that I needed to change my ways so he wouldn't have to hit me. Deep down I knew that it wasn't my fault. I knew I had done nothing wrong, but the compassionate side of me wanted to keep the peace and still wanted to make him happy. And there was a part of me that was beginning to process and believe that it really was my fault why he was like this.

The slightest thing used to get him off, even when it had nothing to do with me. He could be out and someone upset him. Then he could come in and see me plaiting my hair in the living room, and he would beat the hell out of me. I remember I used to wash laundry and then sometimes left the clothes in the machine before I dried them, on the same day though. Anyway, this day he was getting annoyed that when I washed I didn't take them straight out as the machine finished. I mean, he must have wanted me to sit in front of the machine until it finished. Anyway, he had told me a few days before to not do it, and I said I wouldn't, but this day I was busy and didn't get to empty the machine straight away when the machine had finished. He came in and saw the clothes still in there. I heard him come upstairs, all calm and quiet. He even had a conversation with me all nice, and out of nowhere, when I least expected it, bam in my face. Then again in my shoulder and on my arm. The list is endless. This man abused me because I had clothes in the washing machine. I couldn't believe this was happening to me. Why me? I used to cry myself to sleep at night time, and I used to moan and groan to God, asking Him, begging Him, to get me out of this mess I was in. Throughout this season of my life, looking back, I can honestly say that I lost a lot of things: my strength, nearly my mind, my love for family and friends, and my praise, but I never lost my faith in God and my love for Him. The tears that I cried, the heartache and the pain, I was going through it all by myself. I couldn't tell anyone. I was too scared of him. The depression and the oppression—I just couldn't take anymore. Junior's moods used to change like the weather. I could never be sure of what to expect on a daily basis with him. Living with him was like walking on egg shells. I felt like it was hell on earth.

He tried so hard to befriend me and make me feel good. We would live well for long periods of time, but it would never last. I was in an abusive relationship and I felt trapped. I remember back in the days when I used to talk about these things with friends, I would always maintain that it would never happen to me. The first time he hit me would be the last. I would say, "Girl, he wouldn't see me for dust. I would kick the brother to the curb." Well, obviously that is easier said than done. When you're in the situation, the only kicking taking place is him when he's venting his anger on parts of your body whilst you're curled up in the corner like a ball. People, I've been there. And I am here to tell the story, but only because of my faith in God.

One day I came in and his cousin from Birmingham was in the house. Again I saw machinery in my living room that was not supposed to be there. Junior showed me a small gun; it was small enough to be hid in my hair when it was plaited or if I had a weave. He said he wanted me to have it. He got it for me so that if anyone messed with me, I could shoot them. Can you imagine what was going through my head? He wanted me to shoot people! I was shaking. I remember the words stumbled out of my mouth, trying to explain to him I didn't know how to operate a gun and I didn't want it. He said he would show me, and it was in case of need. I knew there were other guns in my house. I didn't know where, but I began to pray again for my safety. Any-thing was liable to happen, and fear filled my heart.

We still, at this point, were travelling to London every week. I found that the trips became more frequent, as we had to spend a lot of time going to see Junior's lawyer, who was dealing with our marriage case for Junior to get his stay in the United Kingdom.

I used to see some breed of money go from our hands into the hands of the lawyer. He wanted me paying for everything, and it wasn't your little five hundred pounds. It was two thousand pounds here and three thousand five hundred there. This money was adding up. The lawyer did what lawyers did best—fill up you head with foolishness and not really do anything. But how were we to know?

One thing about Junior was that he loved witchcraft. Again, it was all new to me, and I knew nothing about it. But one thing I did know is that I was brought up not to believe in it. One day when we were in London, Junior and his mum took me to a house that I had never been to. I felt strange there. As soon as I stepped through the door, it was like the whole atmosphere transcended to something dark and dingy. To the natural eye, every- thing was normal, but alarm bells began to ring in my spirit. I wasn't saved, but the connection with God was still there. I still had the senses that alerted me when something was not quite right. In this man's house, I took a seat reluctantly and watched as the obeah man told my husband about his life—past, present, and future. In the midst of all that, the man turned to me and told about me. He highlighted the fact that I did not believe and then proceeded to tell me about my family life and doings. I was shocked. I had butterflies in my stomach. Everything was true, but I couldn't believe. I knew it was evil spirits manifesting themselves to trap me. On the trip back home to Derby, Junior was trying to convince me of this witchcraft man's authenticity. I explained why I wouldn't allow myself to believe, and he explained that it was not harming anyone and, therefore, it was okay. "O Lord" is all I can say. The more he talked to me and tried to steer me to his way of thinking, the more I was moving on to his side and agreeing with him. A few days and I was hooked. I was so hooked that I started doing the rituals with him and praying the prayer out of this cult prayer book. I knew this was wrong, but this thing was taking over me slowly and surely. I realised that I was going to London more often and buying potions to concoct at my house and incense to summon protection, but not realising I was summoning evil spirits. Junior used to surround the house's outer area with potions and mixtures to keep the law away. He used to burn candles and say prayers regarding his immigration case. He even had spiri- tual baths to wash bad luck off his body and to purify his spirit. Little did I know that, during all this, we were allowing evil spirits from all dimensions to enter into our home. There were enough in there already, and more were readily available to inhabit our space. I used to feel things in my house watching me. I heard things, voices, and I did not realise these were the product of the spirits that were sharing my space. The devil was having a field day in my house, free to roam wherever he wanted and whenever he wanted. What more could he ask for?

It was during this time that Junior had been back to the obeah man and had been fitted for a silver guard ring. You must be asking yourself, What did she just say? You read correctly—a guard ring. Basically, the obeah man would summon a spirit from the dead, normally an Indian spirit, and he would command it to inhabit the ring. He then stuffed the ring with potions and the like and sealed it with a piece of silver. The spirit in the ring was set to protect the wearer and burn his finger in the event of any danger. The only thing you had to do was feed the ring rum. Are you laughing yet? Because I was at the time. You drop the ring in a big glass of rum, and it would drink it. Yeah, right… .

During the time when I was getting closer to my husband, I was getting further away from my parents and family. My friends were already cut off. Junior did not like them, so they had to go. Of course, I had to keep him happy, so I didn't have a choice. The few times I had visited my mum, she was always worried about me. She used to tell me about the dreams and visions she had. Two stand out in my mind. Junior and I were standing at a bus stop, and she was on the bus passing. We were dressed in wedding clothes. Another dream was when she met me on the road and I had loads of layers of clothes on. I kept taking them off. Both of them were basically talking about my marriage and also that I was hiding something. I was so shocked and scared to admit the truth that I continued to deny the fact and continued to lie to her.

Bored in our house, all I did was clean, watch telly, or sleep as I wasn't working at the time. If he was not there, what else could I do? He was happy to be in control of me, knowing where I was at all times so I would stay in line. He knew where I was, but I never knew where he was. And woe was me if I ever asked him. He did not take kindly to me, farcing in his business as it were, whilst he was out there having all the affairs he felt like with different women in Derby while I was home. You may ask me how I knew he was having affairs in Derby. People, come on! Women know these things. Then they always get confirmed when the girls decide to get bright and feisty and let you know they have your man. On one occasion when I asked him about it, he didn't get mad. He was actually sounding scared of the fact I knew one of his secrets. He was sleeping with one of my enemies. He denied it, but, as I said, I am a woman. We feel these things. He was nice to me for so long; no one was more loving than him. We even saw the girl in the street, and he stopped the car and went up to her to cuss her off and kick her down, just to prove to me that she was lying. Men are so wicked.

The girl set out with a vendetta against me. She said she was pregnant, and she wanted her baby's father, which was my hus- band. I remember the day we nearly had a fight when I saw her again. He just sat there in the car, whilst this girl of his was going to fight me about something I knew nothing about. He was weak, probably sitting there scared. She was going to tell me more of his business. That's when I realised he didn't respect me. That's when I realised, no matter what, I had to get out of this relation- ship. The only question plaguing me was how I was actually going to do it, after all I knew it was not going to be easy.

Eventually, she said she lost the baby and blamed me. Everywhere she saw me, she tried to exact war on me. I ignored her and then wanted to tell everyone I made her lose her unborn baby. It pained me to look at him; I loved him, but he was causing me pain and lying about it as well. The thing that burned me most was that we had been trying for a baby for the whole of the year, and then this girl comes along and she's pregnant. That cut me so deeply that I couldn't even bleed if I wanted to. It told me that there was nothing wrong with him. It told me that I was the problem, that I would never be a mother. Can you imagine how it feels to want something, but it would never materialise because of the makeup of your body? I fell into deep depression, and even cried to God about it, but I could not get an answer. Junior even took me to the obeah man that we were seeing in London, and he told us that I had a blocked tube. How he thought he knew that, I don't know. I had been to the hospital for all the tests, and they said everything was fine. So I don't know where he got this blocked tube diagnosis from; he was not a doctor. He mixed a potion for me in a big 750-millilitre bottle, and he said I had to drink it twice a day. It was nasty. I don't know what was in it, but it tasted like poison. After taking it for about two days, I poured it down the sink, because I was just worried about what I was drinking. I didn't know what was in it. That caused another argument. Junior had to pay fifty pounds for the bottle, and then I threw it away. I did not care. All I knew was that I was not drinking it.

Junior used to spend the days at home tormenting me most times, but, as night would fall, he used to be out on the "road" as it were, making money, as he used to call it. I felt like a recluse. I had no friends left in Derby and I felt lonely. Even though someone was around, namely Junior, I was still alone. I was empty inside. I had nothing. Even though I had material things, I felt dead inside. I needed to be revived. I was searching for comfort, and there was a friend I had that lived in London and who did fraud for fun. He had a business and worked fine, but he was heavily involved in the running of defrauding money from anywhere possible. Out of boredom and out of not wanting to depend on Junior, I linked up with him and he set me up with a few fraudulent deals. He used to tell me about all the deals he had done for people worth thousands into millions of pounds, and something inside of me wanted some of that. I was a witness to deals that had gone through for people, so I knew it worked. And I knew it had to work for me.

How wrong was I? I went through a season where I was embarking on all these deals, and everything was fine, until I was to draw the money, attend to the money in some way, and it would just disappear. It would be there all the time and, as I attempted to retrieve it, would just be swallowed up by the bank- ing system. It was like it was being zapped into a black hole. I didn't understand how it worked for other people. I had witnessed it working, but when it came to me, it always went wrong. I remember about twice in the five-year period, a few things went through for me, but nothing groundbreaking. Out of boredom, I could have gotten myself into trouble and ended up in prison, just because I wanted to be needed, maybe even loved. I just wanted some attention and care.

I came to the conclusion that I was a failure in the eyes of my parents. I had started university and didn't finish because I got caught up with the goings on in this world, with relationships and then some. I decided that I would try to get back on the bandwagon and return to university in February 2003. I sorted out the paperwork and enrolled again. Everything was going well, until about four months into the course. I felt so down and depressed again; it was the cycle I went through each year. The depression, the oppression, the stress, the wanting better for myself, but the feeling of being stuck in a trap, a 360-degree trap, going around and around. I was aware of being in these modes; I also knew when I was out of these modes. If somebody had asked me, I could also tell them when the depres- sion started and when it ended. It was predictable like that; I just knew. I was sad, grey inside, and happiness was not for me. At that time, I felt like I was deemed to be miserable for the rest of my life.

This all related back to the choices I had made in my earlier days. They say the choices you make today will form your tomorrow, and I am a living witness to this fact. I made some bad choices a few years previous. I got hooked up with men that were no good for me. I got married against the will of my friends and family and God. And I made various other wrong choices along the way. I was now paying for these choices, one by one. My marriage life was far from perfect, and as much as Junior liked to lie and pretend everything was okay, I couldn't. As much as he used to beat me up, I was one step closer to wanting to commit suicide. The fwwling of wanting to commit suicide was so profound in my life that it was astonishing.

It starts with a smack here and there, till it reaches the point where you can't tell anybody, because you still love him and don't want him to get in trouble—even though he could kill you by what he is doing sometimes. Sometimes the beatings get so bad that you need hospital treatment, but you can't get it because they will question you and get the police involved. Remember, you still love him. So you sit in silence, and you begin to bear it because, of course, you can't fight back. Because if you do fight back, you will make him even angrier, to the point where he could kill you. So you say nothing. When he says you made him do it, you agree until you believe within yourself that you really do make him do it. Then the enemy plays these tricks on your mind. And you reach the point where you are telling yourself that if you are making him do this to you, then you must not be a good person, because you are making him into an evil person when he is good. So if you are the fault, you don't need to be here. So take yourself out. You would not believe the countless times when I would be driving and would hear a whisper in my ear saying, "Put your foot down; no one will miss you. It won't hurt." On countless occasions, I would hear voices telling me to do things that would cause destruction to me, my family, and friends. Put it this way—if I had listened, I could never be here today to tell this, my story.

As much as I still was not where I needed to be in regards to my faith in God, I never ceased to whisper prayers to Him to get me out. Rather, I should say that I used to cry, moan, and groan to Him, begging

Him to work out my mess, to get me out of what deaf ears and a hard heart had put me into. Whether my prayers got answered or not, you won't know unless you read the rest of the book!

In the midst of all of this, as I said beforehand, I was alone. I couldn't go to my family. At this point, they didn't even know I had married, and this was about eighteen months after I had gotten married. I was still hiding it, and even thought they were getting the dreams and visions, I was still denying it. I felt like I was in torment. I wanted so much to sit down with my mum and talk with her. She was supposed to be my best friend. I was supposed to be able to tell her anything, but I was scared. How would I tell my mum, who held me in such high esteem, that I had been lying to her for more than two years, that university flopped, that I was married to this man (or even this terrible man), and that I was on the brink of suicide at the age of twenty? How could I do it? I felt like I had the weight of the world on my shoulders. The only thing was that it wasn't the world's; it was all mine.

4
Depression

Junior had his bad points, but he loved to laugh and play or ramp, as we call it. He loved to ramp to the point that I used to get annoyed and upset. This is because sometimes it used to hurt, and he never seemed to hear when I would beg him to stop. Dur- ing one of the occasions when he had initiated a ramping session, I had figured out that the only way to get him to stop was to dig my nails deeply into his hand. This was now my weapon, so I used it. But it was the worst thing ever. I did not do it on purpose; it was an emergency reaction, because he was hurting me. He shouted at me, "If you dare to dig your nails in me again, I will make you regret it, because I'll scratch you back, but with a metal instrument!" Well, obviously, that shocked me. For a while I started to grin and bear it, until yet again my body reacted to his messing around by digging my nails in his hand. I tried my best but could not refrain; I mean, I was in pain. Once I focused on what I did, I remember I started crying and saying sorry repeatedly. I felt as though I could feel the pain he was about to inflict on me, before he even did it. I knew it was coming, but it did not come straight away. It was actually a few days later when, out of the blue, this man got a metal nail file and just swiped it across my arm. I remember seeing blood. I wanted to pass out, because I am quite squeamish. I started crying and asking him why he did it. All he said was, "I told you don't mess with me."

I don't know if you have realised by now, but it was like I was not dealing with a human being. He seemed possessed. He did not seem like he was on this planet half the time. Maybe he had some mental health issues attributed to the large amount of cannabis he would consume daily. One thing I did know, the praying or talking, as it was, with God became more intense. I had to get out one way or another. Suicide had been ruled out, because I was scared of pain. If I were to kill myself, some sort of pain would have to be inflicted. I would feel something. So, in a way, that fear saved me.

I have so many memories of my past. The majority of them from before the great change are not good and could have killed me. But they did not kill me, because I am still here.

Looking back, I am reminded of one morning when I woke up and Junior was still sleeping—or so I thought. I received a phone call from a male friend (my goddaughter's dad), which Junior did not like. The caller wanted me to meet him and go to town quickly that morning. I did not have a problem with that, as it was a simple request, but Junior found it an issue. He got up and was running a bath; it seemed as if he was standing outside the door when I was making my plans. As soon as

I put the phone down, he came in the room, and from the far side of my bed, I felt the impact of his fist in my face. I was so shocked that I was seeing stars. He started arguing and raring off about me going to town and about people ringing my phone. I thought to myself, You make me cut off my friends and family, and now you don't want anyone to ring my phone. Are you for real? He took my phone and rang my friend back. He sat on the phone with the guy, asking why he was ringing. This is the irony in the situation: the guy was so scared of Junior that he lied and told Junior that I rang him. But Junior was there and had heard when he rang me. So when he got off my phone with my friend, he beat me again because of what the guy said to him.

Over the weeks I had made up with my friend who was my Godson's mother Shereene, and I was due to meet up with her later on that day. I met Shereene later on that day, and I was trying my best to hide the big swollen face I had, which was rapidly going black, but it was not working. I had nowhere to go. I could not go home, because my mum would see. Yet again, I was alone. My friend was threatening to call the police on him, which I could not allow her to do. You might wonder if I was stupid. No, I was not stupid—just still loving my abuser.

Junior got in trouble a few times in the past and continued to get in trouble, but considering what he was deeply involved in, he never got caught. Once when we were driving to Chad- desden, as we passed Pentagon Island in Derby and passed the Derby Cricket Ground, I saw another car driving at me as if it was going to crash into my side; a riot van was behind and in front of me. I was in so much shock that I couldn't even cry. My heart started to palpitate at quadruple speed, and I was speechless. I don't know what the police were thinking, but I was kind of (but not fully) innocent of what was going on. They did not find any Class A drugs on Junior, as (it seems as though) Junior had swallowed them whilst they were telling me to open my door. They opened his door, and he still had a big ganja spliff in his mouth. They took it off him and put it in a forensic bag to send for testing. Then they allowed me to drive to the police station with two officers, whilst Junior went in the riot van. I heard, "Strip search, Mrs. Woodhouse." I was gasping, asking myself why and how I got involved in this mess. I had to go through a degrading search. It made me feel so small, as if I was worthless. Then the police followed me home and came to search my house. Now I was worried about the searching part, because even though I was not sure what was in my house, I knew the kind of man that I lived with and that there were things in the house that should not have been there. They came, they searched, and left. Nothing was found, which Junior later attributed to the voodoo that he was working, but I put it down to the grace of my God.

Junior was cautioned for the cannabis, released, and charged to go to a programme called Addaction, which was a type of counselling group for drug users. Well, as you can imagine, he did not go and thought it did not matter, which it seemed as though it did not … until one Sunday afternoon in early August 2003. Two undercover officers came around to visit him. The excuses they gave were that they were just checking that everything was okay with him and had to give him a formal caution. I thought it was strange that they would come to his house; nor- mally, it would be better and save time to get him to come into the station. I knew their visit was for more than they were letting on, but later down the line, it would have to be revealed.

Junior and I were still having hard times, as we just could not get on. That summer, his family came over from Jamaica for holiday again, but this time he got a house nearby for them to stay in. He was not spending time in our house already, and when they came, I hardly saw him. He would come in morning times, bathe, and be gone again. I would continue to spend my days staring at the four walls or watching rubbish on telly.

I had a friend that Junior got on with—maybe because he was a man—I don't really know. Anyhow, one evening we just went over to Sinfin to see him, and everything was okay and going fine until he started ramping with me again. I fought with my feelings and decided that, even if I am in pain, I need to bear it. Even worse, we were in someone else's house, and I did not want a scene. I scratched him but it was by accident. He did not even say anything to me; he got my car key and swiped me across my belly and my upper back, at that time our friend had gone upstairs for something. It was stinging for a while, and I did not know how bad it was. I literally could not speak. I did not even look at him. I couldn't. I felt like I wanted to run away. I eventu- ally got in the car when we were ready to go, and I drove home in silence. In my head, all kinds of stuff were going on. I think I was trying to process what happened, but I really couldn't. We got home and he spoke to me, but I did not respond. I got ready for bed, and when I looked, the white top I was wearing was full of blood back and front. I was bleeding rapidly and was in a lot of pain, and I had to deal with it. He came to hug me and apolo- gise, and I started to cry. I should not even say cry, because it was more like I started to groan. This man had violated me, and now he was trying to say "sorry" and tell me it was my fault why it happened. Through speaking to God, I was gathering the strength, bit by bit, and he was speaking to me to the point where I could get over it, when this crazy man was telling me that I made him beat me. I no longer believed this, but did not let him know that. He did not need to know that yet; it was not the time to reveal that I was gradually going through a renewal in my mindset.

As the days, the weeks, and months passed, Junior and I were still fighting a lot and arguing constantly. The number of times that I jumped in my car and hit the A52 to Nottingham was multiple. I never knew why I hit the A52. I don't know if it was because, when we lived in Nottingham, it was the happiest time of my life with him, or if it was because I was confused. But one thing I knew was that as soon as I got there, I turned around and came right back home. I remember the car windows used to get so steamed up as I was driving from the tears flowing from within and the groaning because I was in agony from what he had said or done to me.

Around early September 2003, there was a knock at the door. When I opened it, there were two undercover police officers. I instantly got the shakes on, wondering why they were here and what had gone wrong now. My husband was in the bath, so I went up to him and let him know someone was here for him. They waited patiently, seated downstairs in the lounge.

Junior came downstairs, and one of the officers stood to greet him: "Mr. Woodhouse." They introduced themselves and remained standing as one of them asked if Junior would assist them by travelling to the police station to answer some questions in regards to some identity problem they had. One of the officers turned to me and asked me what name I knew Junior by, and I told him. He then asked me if I knew anyone called "Denzel Wesley, born 27 June 1971." In shock, I stuttered, "No," but inside I knew this was the big secret he had been hiding from me. The officer calmly turned to me and said, "Don't worry, love, we will have him back to you in no time." Junior left with the officers, not under arrest or anything, but I knew deep down that I wasn't seeing him again.

He assured me everything would be okay and that they were making a mistake. I reluctantly agreed with him, and he went.

I rang Junior's cousin and told him what happened. He made his way straight over to Derby to be with me; his friend Garfield was already at the house. Garfield was a chatterbox. As soon as I let him know what happened, and what the police had said to me, he started singing like a parrot. He told me everything from A to Z. You must be wondering what happened and what he said. All shall be revealed in the fullness of time, my dear friends.

Seconds, minutes, hours, and days passed. I was not hearing anything, and the police were not very helpful, as they would not release information to me. They just assured me that he was okay and that they still had him. Finally, the phone call came from a distressed man who sounded like he had been crying a lot. I was now speaking to a man who sounded so small, like he couldn't hurt a fly. Suddenly the tables had turned. I was in control, and he was depending on me for his survival.

What would you have done? Left him to rot? Well, if I was heartless, by all means that would have been great but, remember, I loved this abusive, vile man that, for the time being, I was calling my husband. He was able to tell me briefly where they were moving him to and requested that I bring him some clothes quickly, before they moved him. I honoured his request, but I was not able to see him before he went. I was advised that when he got to his destination, I needed to arrange with the prison visiting times. Again I waited a few hours, until he called me when he got to Portsmouth. He didn't have long, but long enough to give me the personal number he had so that I could call him. I left him to settle in a bit and then gave him a ring. The first few weeks I cried a lot, and I actually missed him. I missed this abusive man in my life. I had reached a stage where I didn't want him anymore, but I still preferred for him be there being abusive to me than in an immigration detention centre. It sounds crazy and bizarre, even to me now, as I have moved on. But when you're in love, they say love is blind.

In the detention centre, visits were allowed every day for two hours and then seven hours on Thursdays. You can imagine, he wanted me there every day. How inconsiderate! I mean, I know he was in a predicament, but to drive four hours there and four hours back every day, I would have been exhausted—not to mention the money and time it would cost. Anyway, to keep him happy and keep the peace, I used to go back and forth three times a week, even four if he was lucky. I brought him clothes, resources, money, and cannabis (I know), basically anything he asked for. I looked after him whilst he was in there and kept him happy enough. I had to keep encouraging him and keep his spir- its up. Regardless of what he had put me through, the fact that I felt like I was living in hell on earth had no bearing; because the kind hearted nature within me wouldn't allow me to be evil to him. It would have been easier for me to let him rot and get on with my life, but there was still an element of fear within me that he would get out anyway and then attempt to kill me or something for deserting him.

Looking back at the first time I visited, it was shocking. It was the first time I had ever been to these kinds of places. It was a big Her Majesty's prison that was converted for immigration use. Security was tight: metal detectors, dogs, and big clanging doors. I cried the first few times at the realization that someone I knew and cared about was in this kind of place. Sometimes I used to just stare at him and wonder how he got there, when I say how he got there it was hard for me to accept considering I was just finding out the true story of his past.

Finally, he was ready to tell me the truth, the whole truth. He said that he was always planning to tell me, but he was not ready to tell me yet. He said it was a shame that I had to find out the way that I did. I really have to laugh, as it was more like he was sorry that he got caught.

I did not make Junior (or whatever his name was) aware that his cousin and so-called best friend had already told me every- thing a few days prior to me seeing him again in this situation. I wanted to see if the stories would match up or if he would continue to lie to me. But he didn't; he told me the whole truth.

Junior told me that he had been in England for many years before, and he used to live in London. I had not mentioned this before, but when I met Junior and we were always up and down in London, he knew every place there. He knew various backstreets and short-cuts around London. I always thought it strange, as he was only just supposed to have come in the country in December 2001. Anyway, back to the story in progress.

So he lived in London, and he was a drug dealer in Brixton. He had been doing it for a while and was part of an undercover operation. He was trapped, caught, and arrested. He was sentenced to three years in prison and deported at the end of it. The deportation order stated that he could not enter the country for five years and nine months. When he came in 2001, he was nine months ahead of the deportation order. So he then went on to explain the reason why he came back early and why he changed his name to get back here. Whilst back in Jamaica, his mum bought him a car to run taxi so he could make some money for himself. He employed a close family member to drive for him, and they arranged between them how the profits would go. Anyway, after a while, he was not receiving money from the family member as he was supposed to.

So he told him to bring back his car. He said there was some kind of argument, and he had to take the car back by force. Then one night the car was parked outside his house, and the close family member and his friends came and scrapped the car. They stripped it of tyres, windscreen, and everything else that could be detached. I hope you are able to imagine this. I mean, the bare shell of a car! It's incredible what lengths some folks will go to for revenge.

On waking up in the morning, Junior saw what had happened and got mad. He inquired as to what was going on and who had done this. The way he explained it was that the family member was showing off the fact that he had arranged for this to happen. So Junior made the conscious decision to teach him a lesson, and I do not mean trigonometry. One night, he arranged for a driver to take him to the family member's house, and he went in there and shot up the place and everyone in it. The one thing he did not bank on was anyone surviving, not when they had twelve shots lodged in their body. There was never any proof that it was him, but the family member was linked to the police and judges that were involved in the case. In the end, when it eventually went to court, no amount of obeah in the world could help him. He was sentenced to twelve years in prison. In Jamaica, it is not like the prisons in England. It is a hundred times harder to sur- vive, and they do not do half sentences or early parole for good behaviour. When the judge says twelve years, it is twelve and not one day less.

Junior went on to tell me that he and three other people escaped from the prison. I don't know how they did it, but the first thing his friends did was get him a passport and a ticket off the Island. (This is to cut a long, dreary story very short.) So Junior Anthony Woodhouse was born. To this day, I do not know where he got the name from. He said he made it up, but for all I know, it could be a dead person's name. No one will ever know.

He came to Derby, met me, and the rest, as they say, is history. What a long-winded story, but all true. I made sure to investigate it before I accepted it as being true. I had trusted him once; there was no way I was going to trust him again so easily. So this is who I was married to. I am still trying to work it out now. He was a confused and maybe mentally ill guy who was trying his luck. A great lesson from this is that if you think the government doesn't know everything, you are wrong. He was always so careful not to get in trouble or be in the wrong place at the wrong time, but they still knew. They always find you out. You cannot run or hide; Big Brother is watching.

During the whole ordeal of Junior being incarcerated, I acquired a job as a sales assistant at ASDA WalMart, a large department store and supermarket. I was spending faster than it was coming in, so I needed to get another source of income. At first, as with everything, all was good and I really enjoyed working there. I invested myself into working hard and earning pennies just to pay bills and keep my husband happy. But eventually, the emotion of everything once again caught up with me, and I could not bear it anymore.

In the process of acquiring the job at ASDA, I transferred my university course to Derby University, because, for some reason, I believed that I would be able to handle it better if I was study- ing near home. If the mind is not right, no matter what you try and do, there is no success. I was heavily burdened. Depression and oppression continued to dominate my life, because I allowed them to. I think I fell deeper into depression when I spent my twenty-first birthday at home on my couch with a bottle of champagne. I was crying all night and drinking myself into a stupor. I felt so worthless. Again I was crying out to God, begging Him to release me, to bring me out. I think it was during these times that I found Christian television, and I began to receive my strength by way of the various programmes I used to watch.

My best friend, who Junior hated with a passion, started to come around and decided to stay with me a while whilst Junior was away, just to keep me company. She was a great support, because sometimes the four walls would make me feel like I was going mad.

Again not being able to concentrate because of life worries and also because I had to spend so much time travelling to London to see lawyers for Junior, my studies once more had to take a backseat. It came to the point where I could not even work at my job, because there was just no time. So where would I get money from to live? Do you remember previously that I was introduced to fraud? Well, to stop myself from being broke, I had to revisit this area of my life, which I had buried because it was not working out for me. I was positive and told myself that maybe my luck had changed. I think it was more like wishful thinking on my part. I started doing a few jobs with my Nigerian friend in London. Not all of them, but a few of them, actually came through. I was able to keep my head above water and pay my bills, pay lawyer bills, and keep Junior supplied with money and items he needed.

In our opinion—well, more Junior's opinion—the lawyer was not doing anything. He had heard about another lawyer who had gotten quite a few guys out of where he was, so he wanted to try him out. He sacked his lawyer and employed Mr. Edwards. Again, this was not really a good idea, but he was so desperate to get out of where he was that he would have tried anything. At one point, he said he was going to escape out of there, and I had to quickly remind him he was in England, where those kinds of things would not work.

So I employed this new lawyer, who again charged extortionate prices and did not look like he was doing anything. I used to get books out of the library and information off the Internet in regards to immigration matters. I spent hours finding all the loopholes and working out a case. I was doing the lawyer's job and still paying him. I sent countless faxes to his office with information he could use to fight the case, but because of desperation, money was not an object and we kept on paying him.

Mr. Edwards always assured me that he was doing his best to sort out the case and that he could get him out. He charged for every phone call, every e-mail, every letter, and every fax. This is how the man, a black man, was dealing with his own people in desperation.

Whilst all this was going on, Junior had made friends with a few people in the immigration centre, and he was put in contact with an obeah man in Victoria Falls, Africa. I used to have to buy him phone cards upon phone cards for him to make the calls to arrange business. He used to tell me to send hundreds of pounds at a time to Victoria Falls. Once it was so they could feed the village, as they were to make a ritualistic sacrifice of a lamb for Junior. The brother was going deep into this witchcraft thing, and I was getting dragged down with him.

One day I received a package from Victoria Falls, and it contained little charms and a guard ring for Junior to wear. I began to become a bit weary, because I really did not know what was being sent into my house from unknown sources. But for my husband—anything.

One day when I visited Junior he was down, because he had received a removal notice that was deporting him from this country a few days after I was going to see him. Instantly, I felt the pressure and the pain and knew that he couldn't leave. I needed him to be with me. I was not well at the time. A strange sickness had come upon me, and I was weak to the point where I could not even turn the steering wheel on a power-assisted steering car. The sickness just came on me. I couldn't climb the stairs or anything; it was almost like I was crippled. It was not bad every day but, as I said, out of the blue it came and back into the blue it went after about a week.

The lawyer was contacted, and he said he was doing everything he could to get the flight cancelled. Up to the day he was going, I was so upset. My friend and I drove to the airport. I broke down in tears; I didn't know what else to do. I was calling the immigration department at East Midlands Airport, the law- yer, and Junior, trying to sort this thing out. About twenty min- utes before boarding, the flight was cancelled for Junior. They took him back to HMP Haslar in Portsmouth, and he instantly put in an asylum application, on the instruction of his lawyer. The application had to show why Junior should have been allowed to stay in this country. He had to prove that, if he was sent back, he would be in significant danger in regards to his life being threatened. I do not recall the story he told them, but it worked. His application had to be looked into and, during this period of time, they had to let him out on bail, as he was not a risk to the outside environment. Obviously, they knew he was here on a name that was not his, even though he denied it. I had to stand by him and deny it too, so they slapped a great big bail bond of ten thousand pounds down for him. This was in the event of him running off, the guarantors would lose the money. Where was the money coming from? We did not have this kind of cash lying around. Well, he did, but it was in another country. I didn't. Even though I was getting money from little bank jobs I was doing, it was being spent straight away. I was so down that I would spend whatever was left on anything I could spend it on. I contacted his family in London, and they were able to raise some of the money. Meanwhile, Junior sent for money out of his bank account in Jamaica.

Whilst all this collecting of money was going on, I had been reading a Jamaican paper. In the back, I found a page of psychic reader people from all over the world. I found a lady who lived in America who fascinated me. I decide to call her to find out what she had to say concerning me. She wowed me! I got through to her, and I did not even have to speak. She told me all about myself and then gave me a chance to ask questions. She gave me information no one could know and answered my questions all correctly. I was shocked to the point that I was not bothered anymore that it was evil spirits manifesting themselves. At one point, she told me to stack four hundred pounds worth of twenty pound notes together and sleep on them. I honestly do not remember why I was doing this, but I will never forget what she told me the next day when I called her back.

"Okay, now send me the four hundred pounds via Western Union."
I thought to myself, Whaaaaaaaaaaaaaaat?

I got angry thinking this was another con artist, and when I related it all back to Junior, the idiot told me to send it to her. I had to ask him if he was crazy, but he was serious. He wanted me to send her the money, so I did in pain. As they say, easy come, easy go.
As time progressed, the lawyer was trying to urge immigra- tion to accept the offer and release my husband on bail. They were so slow; they had no sense of urgency at all. I had to makesure they did not forget

about him, so I faxed and called them every day. By the time I finished, the whole of immigration in the region knew about Junior Woodhouse, as I involved the secretary of state and local Member of Parliaments. The lawyer wasn't doing it, so someone had to.

I remember the day we got the news that they accepted his application and were going to release him on bail. They required him to sign on every Monday at the local police station. We were over the moon—ecstatic! I was so glad my baby was coming home to me. I had missed him so much. I loved him so much. I made up in my mind that I was going to hold him so tightly and never let him go. That was deep. Since he was away, he seemed to appreciate me more and love me more. But that was because I didn't leave him in there to rot.

So Junior was coming home. It was my heart's desire, and I felt like my life was finally getting back on track. They said it would take about a week to sort out and process his release papers. That delay did not bother me, as long as he was coming home. In the midst of all this, Shereene was still staying at my house and getting quite comfortable.

One night it was late and we were going to bed. She normally slept in the spare room, but on this particular night, I had lit a candle and said my prayers or incantations, whatever you call them, and blown it out. I went into my room to bed, and I heard a high-pitched scream coming from the corridor in between the two rooms. My friend came running into my bedroom, shouting that she was not going to sleep in that room, and she jumped into my bed. When she calmed down, I asked her what was wrong. She said she saw a big black cloud moving from the room I had lit the candle in, and it was just hovering in the corridor. Of course, as much as I used to go on as if I wasn't scared of anything, fear instantly gripped me. I just dug deep down under the sheets in the bed and tried to get to sleep quickly.

The next day, I called Junior and was telling him about it, but he was not surprised. He said that it was evil trying to get me, because someone had sent a spell for me. I mean, come on, really! Truthfully, looking back and remembering all this spirits and obeah business makes me laugh now. I am not saying that it is not real. All I am saying is that it is an area that is illegal, and we should not be getting mixed up in it.

Through everything I had experienced—the hurt and the lies Junior had told me—some people would have up and left him, kicked him to the curb. But there was that spiritual tie or bond between us that just wouldn't break and seemed to get stronger. My life has been turned upside down by him, yet I was standing by him. He had beaten me black and blue in the past, but I still loved him. He had cheated on me with other women, but still I trusted him. It just didn't make sense. Why was I acting as if this man had something over me? The answer to that question, in fact, was nothing. He made me feel as if he loved me, when I felt unloved. He made me feel safe, when I felt as if everything around me was sinking in sand. I could go on all day about how he made me feel, but the truth about it was that none of it was real. To me it was as fake as him being called Junior Woodhouse. To me it was a sham to get what he wanted out of the system. The only thing was that he had to use me to access those things. Being on the outside now, if it was my friend in that situation, I would see it. But they say love is blind. I was in the thick of it and did not see a thing. According to my thinking, everything was okay. I had rose-coloured glasses on. I only saw what he wanted me to see and it seemed great.

It was a few days before Christmas, and Junior called me early in the morning. "Babes, can you come and get me? I am coming home today."

I jumped out of my sleep! I was so happy that I didn't know what to do with myself. I had so much planned for my day, but it all got thrown down. Junior was coming back, and I was going to get him. They said they were sorting him out and that he should be out by eleven o'clock a.m. Well, it was eight o'clock a.m. when he called me so I had to get going. I put my foot down on the gas in the car and drove like an F1 racer. I was going to get my baby; nothing was sweeter.

I reached Portsmouth in two hours and picked Junior up from the harbour that was close by. I remember tears came to my eyes. He was free! I saw him and I cried. My heart felt like it was breaking. He begged me not to cry, but I could not help it. I was so happy that I could not contain it. All the months of fearing that he would never be home; all the nights I cried to God to release me, but to release him also. Finally, he was in front of me, free as a bird.

We got on really well for a month at most—it could have even been less. Everything was going well for a while. He tried to make up to me the times when he had lied to me. And me, being gullible, accepted and received him always with open arms. He promised never to leave me again and that he wouldn't beat me up anymore. I was always a fool in my former days.

You may ask why I believed his promises, because when a man who loves to beat women says he will not beat anymore, unless he has been through some kind of counselling or something to break him out of it, he will return to it. Here I had this man promising never to beat me again. I mean, the last time he stabbed me with a car key! But, no, I forgave him and believed his lies.

Eventually he started getting back into what he used to do, selling drugs on the streets and keeping me behind closed doors. The routine soon set in again like rigor mortis. He was out till five o'clock a.m.; sometimes he didn't come home at all until one o'clock p.m. the next day. This was the life we had returned to. Maybe I would pass him on the street, not seeing him since the day before. A simple hi-and-bye life was now what we had.

The only time we seemed to spend time together was when he decided that the house was too quiet, so he would start beating me up again. I mean, can you imagine this man? He was quite sick in his head, by all means, but didn't believe it or wouldn't accept it. Either way, he was off his rocker.

The first beating he gave me after a few months of quietness was with a wooden spoon. I am sure that somewhere in this man's stupid thinking he thought I was a child. I mean, wooden spoons were what they used to beat black kids years ago. Even though I didn't get the spoon when I was young, I got the vacuum end. Not to jump from one thing to another, but I recollect that I was about eleven or twelve years old, and I had done something wrong. My mum was waiting to punish me. All of a sudden she pounced. She grabbed the nearest thing, which was the long vac- uum arm that you vacuum up with, and she swung for me. "Ah!" I said to her. "You missed me …" I was being feisty to my mum, on top of the beating she was out to give me. I was so brave. She dived for me again and missed. I started running and so did she. I ran up the stairs, and as I was going up, she caught my heel. But I kept running and so did she. My brain was in overdrive. I didn't know where to go. I was being cornered; she was going to get me. Instantly, something in my mind said, The bathroom. I picked up speed, ran in the bathroom, and sat behind the door. She was trying to push the door open, but I then remem- bered that the bathroom door had a lock on it. I slid up the door, trying to keep the pressure on so she couldn't get it, and I locked the door.

"Ha-ha! You can't get me now, so you can stay out there," I said to my mum. I was in the bathroom and she was out there, so she couldn't get me. Obviously, I had not really thought this through, as I had to come out there sometime and, when I did, she would be waiting. But what the hay? I had a few hours in there, at least, before my dad came from work and needed to get in there.

So back to the wooden spoon drama. He hit me with the wooden spoon. He totally caught me off guard. He was just talking to me nicely one day in the house and, as I turned my back, he attacked. Bam on my right arm. I turned to him, looking at him in disgust, and he had the nerve to do it again. He promised that he would beat me to death if I didn't do the ironing. Can you believe it? I had to wash his clothes, clean the house, cook, be subjected to imprisonment, and take beatings—and he really wanted me to iron his dirty, nasty clothes, which I had bought for him anyway! This man was a joker, and I refused to do it. Since he had gone and come back, I was getting braver. I decided a long time before that I was going to fight back, that no man would ever do to me again what Junior had done to me. I made up my mind that if I died in the process, at least I would die fight- ing. Crazy! So I refused, and he said no more about it. He left the house in silence, and I didn't see him till the next day.

Slowly but surely, I used to hide from him and call my friends, making excuses to go out of the house. You may say, "Well, he wasn't there anyway, so what difference did it make?" Well, a lot. He always had tabs on me. It was just my luck to leave the house and have him see me, get mad, and decide to slap me up in front of people and send me home.

That's when it would get dodgy, because at home, when no one was looking, I could chat back to him and maybe get away with it, as with the wooden spoon. But if I attempted it on the streets in front of people that were scared off him, it would have been a different story. Maybe I wouldn't even make it home, because he would have to show me up for the sake of his reputation. The thing is, after all this, he would say "sorry" to me behind closed doors. Argh! The ways of the underworld—just disgusting.

I started going back to my mum's church occasionally. I had fallen back into that deep depression, which so easily beset me, and I needed help. I needed God. There was a guy at the church that I knew from the streets. He was gay, and I was not a fan of gay people. You can ask any Jamaican about them, and you will hear profane language, which I could never repeat, even if I was still in the secular world. The guy was a Jamaican also, which was weird, but he loved men. I knew this, but he had everyone in the church fooled. He thought he could fool me, because he did not want me to tell people. It had gotten to the point in my life where I was sick of keeping secrets for people. I could no longer stand the fact that this man was in church, pretending and lying to people. So I told someone. Maybe it was the wrong move. Maybe that's where I should have taken myself out of the picture. Maybe I should have just moved along and gone on like I did not see. But how could I? It was as if he was taking God for an idiot.

You can fool man, but let me tell you one thing, you cannot fool God. No matter how hard you try and how deep you hide, you cannot hide from Him or fool Him. So why would you even try? The person I told was concerned deeply about the revelations I had given her and made a few phone calls, which, in turn, came back around to the guy.

And my name was big in the thick of the mix-up. I revealed his secret, and he was on the warpath—on the rampage. He was acting as if he was going to draw my blood. All of the things that I had done for him in the past, the financial help I gave him when he had no one else—none of it mattered now. He was going to get his revenge, and he wanted to make sure he brought me down.

One day I received a call from my mum, and she asked me to come see her at home. I was scared at the time, because of the tone of her voice and the questions she was asking me over the phone. When my mum acted like that on the phone, it usually meant I was in big trouble. So I set a time with her. I put her off a few days, because I really did not want to deal with it. But I had to eventually.

The day came and I went to see my mum. Oh, Lord, I wanted to cry and maybe, at the time, die. After all these years of lying to my parents and denying the fact of marriage when I was asked, my judgment had finally come. I could not hide anymore. I could not lie anymore. My parents knew everything, and I would be only digging a bigger hole if I attempted to lie. Well, I would be, but I had to try. I started out by denying everything that was said and attempted to clear my name by reiterating that the only rea- son he was saying all this was because of his condition and the fact that I exposed him. It was not working. My mum had what you might call "a discerning spirit." She knew when I was lying, and she was not taking it from me anymore. I started to cry at the realisation that she did not believe me, until the crying turned into groaning. The groaning meant I could not take this any- more. The groaning meant I was sorry and I needed help. My mum was worried and begged me to tell her what was going on and what was wrong, but I felt like I was in so much pain. I felt like I had the world on my shoulders. I wanted to give up the ghost, but I couldn't. At this point, I definitely wanted to kill myself again, but I couldn't. I was at the point of my parents losing all trust and faith in me. I thought that once I had finished telling them the events of the past three years, our relationship would be in complete disrepair. I knew it and did not want to face it.

Nonetheless, I admitted it. I admitted to the fact that I was in a relationship and married to this man, but I did not tell them everything. By the time I was finished, there was a sickening silence. My mum could not speak; she was trying to process the information but was dumb-struck. She broke down and cried. It was all she could do. I had let her down big time, and she couldn't handle it. She was finding it so hard to digest the information download that I had given her. She looked like she was in pain. This was just the wedding I told her about, and she was acting like this. What if I had told her I was in an abusive relationship and that he sold drugs? Oh, and that he had been locked up for months because he was illegal, and his name was not real. No, I worked out that I could not subject her to more misery. So I kept all that information to myself. I had to go through all of this with her, and my dad was not even there. So I had to go through it all again with him, too, and her again. The bonus at the time was that I did not live there, so it was easier. I could avoid him for as long as possible.

I was heartbroken when I left my mum's house, not knowing what to do with myself. I went home in despair. An empty house, just me and the four walls. I felt like my heart was bleeding. I called Junior and he came home. I told him what happened and how it came about, and he seemed to be happy about the whole thing. His remarks were something to the effect that, if they knew, we wouldn't have to hide anymore and the lies could stop. My mum called again. I was scared to answer, but he urged me to. She told me that Junior had to come to the house, as they had to meet him formally and get introduced. I told him and they set a date. I decided within myself that I would probably have to take painkillers to numb the pain of the day that was to occur. I had not seen my dad yet. He had heard and had been to my house, but I ignored the door. I could not face him. I was scared of my dad. I could never lie to him. He always saw right through my lies. I would always start crying when he spoke to me. He never slapped me; he never had to, even as a child. All he had to do was speak. He had the authority in his voice. He was serious, and he didn't mess around.

The day of judgment arrived; it was meet the parents. Have you seen the film that has the same name, starring Ben Stiller? Well, it was not exactly like that. It was worse. We entered the house. The atmosphere was so tense that it could have been cut with a knife. Junior and I sat in the living room in opposite chairs. It felt wrong for me to sit next to him, so I didn't. I sat next to my dad, and he did not have a smile on his face. This was a family meeting, my first in the history of my days on earth. I didn't know what to expect, but I knew it was nothing good. My dad did the long speech of how precious I am to God, and what they went through for me to come here. He told Junior that I was a miracle, that I am marked by God, and that God would not allow anyone to come and mess me up in life. I knew my dad was mad and did not approve of him. He did not speak to me once. Everything was directed at Junior: how he was so wrong to do what he did and that he would pay. Well, not exactly in those words, but you can imagine. I saw change in Junior that day, but only for that time. He was so humble and fearful of my father and what he said. He was careful not to offend him, even though I knew he didn't like him. Junior warmed more to my mum, and vice versa. They got on well that it was as if he was her child and I wasn't. I am reminded of occasions when Junior and I would have dis- agreements and he would ring my mum and tell her things and it always appeared as if she believed him.

Junior's humbleness was short-lived. By the time we reached home, we were up in arms and arguing again. Nothing had changed between us; the fact that I had just sat in front of my parents and lied meant nothing to him. I lied to protect him, but he couldn't care less. Well, I would have liked to see how he would have dealt with my dad if I had told them that he was beating me up.

One day, I received a random call from Clive. Do you remember Clive from earlier on in my life? He was still hoping to get back with me, but I explained to him that I was married and committed now, to which he sounded hurt. Anyway, he said he had a big drugs link and he was willing for Junior to get the drugs he had, if he bought him a plane ticket; they could do business together. I had never had a reason to not trust Clive. He was always so honest with me. How was I supposed to know he had changed? They both went into deep business with each other. I wasn't really involved, because I was beginning to feel nervous around those things. All I knew was that Junior sent a lot of money to Clive in Jamaica for him to come to England with these drugs he had stolen.

Things were going well until Clive received the last amount of money and then we didn't hear from him again. We called him. We got people in Jamaica to call him, and nothing. Clive had skanked Junior, and now Junior was on the warpath. At one point, he was blaming me and telling me I had to pay him back all his money, because it was my friend who stole his money.

The day that Clive was supposed to come, Monday, 16 August 2005, came and Junior had to sign on at the police station first. He was determined to go to the airport to see if he had still come, even thought we hadn't heard from him in more than a week.

Junior left early that morning to go and sign on at the police station, and it was the last time he ever stepped out of our home door. Time was running late, and I began to get worried when I was calling him and he wasn't answering his phones. I decided to drive down to the police station, and when I did, his car was parked up in the car park. I sat out there for a while—a while being two hours—and then I decided to go in and find out what was going on. They wouldn't tell me much. All they said was that he was in custody and immigration had him.

It wasn't until around seven o'clock p.m. when they let him call me. That's when I found out that they had a flight date for him on

Wednesday, and they were going to send him to Jamaica. Just like that, no warning, nothing. Instantly, I got onto the lawyer, but all he wanted was more money. He wasn't actually doing anything, just wasting our time. Junior called a new lawyer who was with legal aid, as we decided he wasn't going to waste any more money on lawyers and this case. So we sacked the previous lawyer and went with this new one. He was ever so good and always tried to help in the best way he could and in whatever capacity.

He got the flight stopped and started with the appeal process. I had to make quite a few trips to London and, at one point, our case was at the Old Bailey in London. The Old Bailey is one of the biggest Courts in the United Kingdom which hosts many big trials and cases. We tried everything and still were spending a profound amount of money on the proceedings.

Yet again, days turned into weeks and weeks turned into months. Junior was locked up in another immigration detention centre, and I was up and down the motorway four days out of seven to visit him. As was usual in these situations. all of the bills fell on my shoulders and petrol wasn't cheap, as well as having to give Junior money where he was. It wasn't easy. The only money I had to live on was the eight thousand pounds that I had gotten back from the solicitor—and Junior had sent half of it to Jamaica to sort out some business for himself.

The new lawyer that we employed to try and help Junior did his best, but nothing was working. We had to prove that Junior wasn't who immigration said he was. All of the evidence was in his favour at that point. He even spent day and night filing down his fingertips, as we had to hire a fingerprint expert to analyse and take his prints. Even though we did all this and spent more than three thousand pounds on the case, it still failed, because immigration didn't use the fingerprints freshly taken by the expert. They used the ones on file, which defeated the object of taking prints anyway.

It was obvious that we wouldn't win this case against the state, so it was pointless continuing to waste money trying. One day I made the suggestion to Junior that he go home to Jamaica, and then I would file for him properly. It was a suggestion made by the lawyer previously, a suggestion that I never wanted to happen, but I was at my breaking point. My money was nearly finished, and I needed to get my life on track. I couldn't keep liv- ing like this forever.

The way things were going, he could have been in there for a long time. Just because they had let him out the first time didn't mean they would let him out again. It had been five months and not one bit of progress. I was giving up and just had to convince him on my theory. We alerted immigration of our decision and then just waited for them to give him a flight date. It was at this point that I told my parents some of what was going on. I couldn't let them into the fullness of the story, as I still didn't want Junior to look bad. So I told them part truth and part lie. Basically, as far as they knew (well, up until now), he was arrested for working when he wasn't supposed to, and so they sent him home because of it. It was only later on when my mum used to argue with me about it that I would get angry, and things would come out of my mouth about him lying and not being who he said he was. I didn't want to lie, but I think I even told her eventually that he married me in a name that wasn't his. I don't actually remember, but anyway, moving on.

The day came when he was going to Jamaica. I actually remember that I was crying on the phone to him. He had a mobile, so he called me when he was at the airport. We talked for a long time. We were both worried about what would happen when he reached Jamaica, but we were hoping for the best.

During the whole time, I never heard from Clive again. Can you believe that he stole our money and got off? Never to be seen or heard from again—how rude.

He arrived in Jamaica and everything went well. He instantly went into hiding in the hills or something like that, as he was wanted in Jamaica. If he was caught, he would have been taken straight back to prison, and he didn't want that. I would have felt so sorry for him if anything bad had happened to him, even though he was so evil to me.

5
When you hang with fools

Whilst Junior was in Jamaica, I spoke to him quite frequently. I still loved him strangely enough, but looking back now; I think it was still the fear that was gripping me and even though during the time he was away from me I had slowly come to the realisa- tion that he wasn't for me and that he was using me, I couldn't allow him to feel as if I wasn't going to help him get back to England.

It was so hard for me to leave him. When you love someone, it's hard to let him go. It's hard to come to terms with the fact that it will never get better. But how far do you go? When he is out of your life, why would you invite him back in to continue ruining your life? You don't want to hurt him, but what about all the times he hurt you? What about the times he beat you up until you felt lifeless and then left you for dead?

The memories came flooding back, and even though I found

myself on the phone to him telling him I loved him, it was so hard. One part of me did love him. After all, he was my husband. The other part of me would have gone to prison for killing him.

I was trying so hard to get my life back to normal, but I felt like I was failing. I fell into deep depression, and I still felt as if I didn't want to live anymore.

While driving around, even just to the end of my street, I would hear voices in my head telling me not to stop the car at the intersection, to just keep driving and run into the houses, killing myself. The voices would go on to tell me that it wasn't anything big, no one would miss me, no one would care. So what if I was gone? I would be less stress to my parents. But again, it was the fact that I might have been in pain that kept me from doing it.

I was planning another job bank job with my Nigerian friend Lawrence from London in July of 2005. For some reason, I felt so uneasy about the whole thing. I remember it was around the fifth of July, and I was arranging my train tickets for me and a friend to go down to London on the seventh.

It was the morning of the seventh, and my train was at three minutes after one in the afternoon. I turned my television on at about nine fifteen a.m., and to my shock, horror, and disgust I was seeing reports of the London bombing. The areas that were affected were the same areas that I was supposed to be in later that day. I was sitting there watching these things happen and I couldn't believe it. You can imagine, I was gripped to my seat. I couldn't utter a word, and all I kept thinking about was the fact that it could have been me caught up in that entire travesty. I had to thank God I was safe, but I was hurting inside for the people who were caught up in the destruction that was taking place.

I spent the whole day in front of the television, watching the events gradually unfold. My sisters and other family and friends lived in London, so I was sending texts to as many people as I had contacts for, to make sure they were all safe.

What would posses these people to do this? To destroy life and say it was in the name of their God? Why would a God require sacrifice of life? Why would a God command its followers to kill people? It just showed me the way people can get caught up in religion and interpret religious teachings and readings to mean what they want it to mean.

That job I was doing went down the drain, because I decided that I wasn't leaving Derby to go to London for anything. I valued my life more and, at the time, it wasn't safe to travel to London, let alone by train or bus or even car.

As the days and weeks went on, I was going about daily life, picking up the pieces of what Junior had left behind. The atmosphere in my house was feeling strange. I was there alone, but oftentimes I felt like someone or something else was there with me. I didn't realise the danger I was in. The thing is, when you mix with evil spirits and mess around with dimensions unknown to the natural human limitations, you open doors to all sorts of things that can affect you. Remember, I didn't believe in witchcraft, but I still got mixed up in it until the point when I believed for Junior's sake. I had to believe, as I was made to think that if I didn't believe, he couldn't be set free. That was a load of old rubbish. I had gone into dimensions and said incantations and spells and had opened up my heart and home to whatever wanted to enter in. The fact that I was feeling something present with me and watching me was no joke.

I was a person who usually did not get sick; I didn't even suffer from flu. So when I fell ill suddenly within hours, I knew something was wrong. I started to get really bad headaches and the feeling as if my head was cloudy came over me, then I was finding it hard to breathe, my limbs were sore, and I couldn't make it up a flight of stairs. To work or move was a struggle, and to talk was painful. I was partially paralysed; I didn't know what was going on. The first time it happened, I was home alone for more than a week. I couldn't move. I couldn't even call my mum to tell her what was going on in my life. I spoke to Junior, and he sounded as if he was as shocked as I was. But looking back now, I am not so sure. I remember him telling me of a story about when he was younger and the same kind of thing happened to him. His dad took him to a spiritual healer, and they said he had a spirit on him that was sent to him by way of a witch doctor. I couldn't believe what I was hearing, but I wasn't in the appropri- ate state to hold any sort of conversation with him.

These symptoms went on for about one week. I remember waking up one morning, and I was fine. It was as if I was never sick. Time went on, and I went about my daily life again, until about two weeks later—I remember it was a Thursday evening— and I was driving around a roundabout, when all of a sudden out of nowhere, I went weak at the car steering wheel. I couldn't turn the car. I nearly crashed. I don't know how the car went around and parked. I was so weak, I didn't know what was going on. I felt so ill. It was hard for me to breathe. I started sweating and overheating, and again felt paralysed.

I didn't know what was going on; I was hurting. About half an hour after parking, I felt that if I was quick, I could make it back home. I put my foot down and got home as quickly as I could before the pain got more intense again. It was gradually coming back, and I just managed to get home, bathe myself, and sort my room out to get the things around me that I needed, as I knew when this thing that was happening to me got intense, I was unable to function.

The symptoms came back and I felt like I was dying. I remember calling my mum and letting her know what was going on, because I was on the way to see her when I fell ill again.

She advised me to get rest, but she didn't realise what I was going through and how much I was hurting. During this time of illness, I didn't understand what was going on in my life. I didn't know where this attack of sickness was coming from, but I didn't believe it was natural. I knew that if I ever made it to the doctor's, he wouldn't find anything wrong with me. Something deep down was telling me it was more than normal sickness. After one week, again I was well and again it was as if I had never been sick.

While remembering the story Junior had told me about when he was sick and was taken to a witchdoctor, all that was on my mind was, What if he had gone to a witchdoctor in Jamaica and cast a spell on me? It was strange how I was sick and then well, and then exactly two weeks later on the same day, I was sick and then well a week later again. I couldn't explain it, but I didn't say anything to anyone—least of all, Junior.

My best friend decided to come and stay with me a while, along with her son, which I appreciated more than she knew. I enjoyed being alone sometimes, but this was not the time. I was going through something that words could not explain, so I needed someone with me. One day when I rang Junior, I was walking up the stairs at the time of the conversation and was shocked to hear him tell me that he went to a witchdoctor to find out about me and what I was doing. I failed to understand why he would do this. He said everything was fine, but I know he was lying. This just confirmed my fears that maybe he sent sickness on me, as crazy as it seems. And, yes, I know he is not God, but he was messing around with spiritual things that could affect me.

I started to go out of the house and once more attempt to get on with my life, when I came across a young man one day. His name was Joseph and he was from London. He was in Derby for a few months, working as a builder. He was like a new burst of happiness in my life. We spent all of our time together when he wasn't at work, and he generally made me happy.

It was one step forward to trying to erase the memory of Junior out of my head. Joseph made me think about my future, of things to come, and things I wanted to be doing. During the time I was with him, which was about four months whilst he was here, I hardly spoke to Junior. In fact, I could probably count the number of times I called him on both hands. I knew he felt the vibes, and I knew he knew I was seeing someone, but I wasn't fearful. I didn't care. He was half way around the world and I was happy.

As time went on and we were getting semi-serious, he was feeding me all the lies that men do and making all the sweet promises to keep me at his side, to keep me sucking up to him and directing all of my time and attention to him. I don't under- stand why I always seemed to attract the wrong sort of man— always out for something, always managing to feed me their lies, and I believe them. Was I that gullible and vulnerable? What was I looking for that enabled me to keep falling into these traps?

Was it the belief that, yes, I had been hurt before, but maybe this one was different? God only knows, but one thing I knew was that it was happening all over again.

Joseph promised me that he would try and get his contract extended for him to stay in Derby with me. He also said that he really wanted kids, that he thought he had found the perfect mother for his baby in me, and so on and so forth. He knew all the lines, and I was falling for them hook, line, and sinker.

It wasn't until his contract ended and he was moving back to London that I realised this thing we had going wouldn't last. He was trying to encourage me to travel down to London often to see him. I asked him why I had to follow him up and down, as if I was the stupid one. I couldn't see why we couldn't meet half- way. He could come here one time, and I could go there the next. He was just taking and expected me to continue giving.

He was in London for a few weeks and, even though we spoke often on the phone, I knew something was wrong. After a while, we started talking less and less, until we stopped talking altogether. I slowly forgot about him, and I suppose he forgot about me. It wasn't until a friend of mine went to see him in London and came back to Derby that I found out he was married and lived with his wife.

I was broken. I was in pieces. I had forgotten about this man and didn't care about him anymore, but when I heard this news I was more than shocked. All of the lies he had told me just came flooding back to me, one by one. I was hearing every word he told me amplified in my head, lie after lie. The state I was in around that time was unstable because of all that I had been through with Junior. I just wanted to be loved. He lied to me; he told me he wasn't even in a relationship, let alone married to someone.

I asked my friend for his number. I didn't know what I was going to say to him. I just wanted to hear his voice. I wanted to hear what he was going to say to me.

"Hello," I said.

"Hello … Who's that?" he asked.

"Don't you know my voice by now? Come on, what's wrong with you?"

"Oh, Lee, how are you doing? You all right? It's been a long time!"

"Yes, so what have you been up to? How come you haven't called?"

"Well, I have been really busy working. So when you coming down to see me? I really miss you, you know."

"Why are you lying? You don't even remember me." "Oh, come on, Lee, you know I miss you."

"Be careful, you don't want your wife to hear." "What are you talking about? Wife?"

"Well, I heard you were married and that you didn't want the person who told me to tell me …"

The conversation went on and on. He denied everything and claimed that whoever had told me was just trying to cause trouble between us. But considering there was no us, it was not my problem anymore. I needed to call him for closure, just to see if he would tell me the truth or lie to me. And, yeah, he did; he lied all the way.

I soon forgot about this saga in my life as I started going out raving again. There was a guy named James that I kind of liked. He had tried to talk to me the year before, but I wasn't interested. Back then, it was all about Junior, and I didn't care about anybody else. At this time, some problems had kicked off with the police, and a family member of his got arrested. He wasn't the kind of guy to stick around, and he needed somewhere to stay. Well, I was not the kind of person to say "no"—if I had the room, you were welcome.

He and his friend stayed at my house a few nights, until it turned into a few weeks. Can you imagine how full my house was two guys, two girls and a little boy, that's funny it could have been a movie title. When I initially agreed, it was to the few nights until they got somewhere else to go. Because they were drug dealers, and after many years living with a husband who did this, I didn't want to get involved with anyone else, especially doing these things and staying at my house.

In and out, in and out—they were always in and out. It was obvious that people would start to watch them, because I never caused trouble. I was a good neighbour. No one had any problems with me, and all of a sudden these men were going in and out of my house. Of course it would appear strange.

One morning I got up early to take my godson to nursery and James came with me. I drove up the road to turn the car, as I lived on a street that was a dead end, and when I was driving down, I saw an undercover officer park at the bottom of my street and get out of his car, as if he was going somewhere.

This was the same officer that I had seen a few days earlier going into a house on my street. I was unsettled by this; I knew something was going to happen. I was uneasy, and I had the feel- ing to go and stay at my mum's house for a while.

About two days later, I received a letter from my bank. They were letting me know that they had closed my bank account. They didn't give me a reason and it stipulated in their terms and conditions that they didn't have to tell me why either; but they had three thousand pounds that they needed me to collect, as it was the closing balance. I was shocked by this, because I didn't have any money when the account was open. You can imagine how happy I was; nobody reached the bank quicker than I did that day. They counted out three thousand pounds into an enve- lope and when I walked out of that bank, the idle spirit set in straight away. My friends and I went and bought new mobile phones, clothes, and trainers. By the time I had finished, I had eight hundred pounds left and didn't know what to do with it.

Since I was feeling uneasy, something was urging me to look for somewhere else to live. My friends who now seemed to be permanent lodgers with me suggested we find a house where we could all move in together. At the time I didn't mind. I just wanted to be out of my house. So we went house hunting until we found someone with a five-bedroom house for rent. The rent was eight hundred pounds per month. I paid the new landlord the eight hundred pounds, and he said that I could pay the other eight hun- dred pounds for the deposit at a later date.

I really didn't mind. There were enough of us, and we were all able to do things to get the house sorted out.

They all helped me to pack up everything, and we got a removal date. At the time, I owed my current landlord rent because there were problems with the house. I had to pay to get boilers and other things fixed because he wouldn't. I refused to pay him rent, though, because it would be as if I was paying twice. The night we were moving my things out, we tried to be careful so he wouldn't find out, but it was too good to be true. Halfway through loading up the van, he walked down the street and started asking what was going on.

We tried to fob him off, and my friend even told him that she had bought furniture from me, as I was getting new furniture, and she had to move it for delivery the next day. He was having none of it. All he knew was that I owed him money, and he wanted it before I scarpered. I made an arrangement to sort the outstanding money out with him the next day, just to get him to leave me alone and let me continue to pack up. But of course, I had no intention of paying him.

I was torn that night about where to stay, the old house or the new house. If it was the old house, I could have packed more things up. But if it was the new house, I could have started cleaning. James, the guy which just seemed to attach himself to me, didn't feel comfortable staying at the old house, so we all agreed that we would bog down on the floor at the new house and then go back for the rest of the things the next day.

Considering that we slept on the floor in a strange house, we had a good night and woke up early to get back to the old house for the rest of my things. The guys got a phone call; the message was that my house had been raided. I didn't believe them, because they always made jokes of serious matters, and they were laughing when they told me. All of a sudden, they got serious and were try- ing to drill into me that my house got raided. I couldn't believe it.

I called a taxi straight away, and my friend Shereene and I went to the old house. We were not sure what was going on, so we made the taxi drive to the top of my street and come back down. On the way up the street, a young lad who lived near my house stopped me and told me what had happened that morning. My worst fears had been confirmed. My house had been raided for drugs, something that had never happened to me in my life, something that these two guys had brought my way and now I had moved into another house with them. Shereene had to climb through an open window, because the front door was boarded up. I couldn't get in the back, as I had left my keys in the kitchen. She climbed in and let me in through the back door. I couldn't believe it. My house was upside down, papers everywhere, and everything was ruined. I didn't even know where to start. I had gone to pick up the rest of my things, and now I had more work to do because they had turned out everything.

I had so many things that I had to make a crucial decision, which I found so hard. I had to take the important things and leave the rest. I couldn't afford to have the landlord come and find me in the house. It wouldn't be long until he heard what happened, because he lived at the top of my street. We made a few trips between the houses dropping off things, until the last time, when we got back to the old house and the landlord was there changing the locks. You can imagine how mad he was. All he wanted was his money and to never see me again. Shereene had the gift of gab, and she was chatting with him and trying to hold him off whilst we got more things out of the house. The taxi was full for another run, and I sent it for the guys to unload and come back. When it came back, I was loading as the landlord approached me and stated that he shouldn't be letting me take my things out of the house, in case I don't pay him. The perfor- mance I was about to give would have won me an Oscar.

After much talking, I managed to trick him yet again into believing that I had an appointment with the bank at one p.m. to get the money I owed him out of my account. He believed me. Even I wouldn't believe myself after the run around I gave him, but he did. There was so much to get out of the house, and one p.m. was approaching rapidly. I decided that the wardrobes, cooker, chest of draws, tables, settees, washing machine, dryer, and the other big objects (the majority of them new) had to stay. There was no way the landlord was going to let me back into the house to get my things again, because he wasn't getting any money.

The last time we left the house, we told him we would be back in twenty minutes with the rent. It was the last he was going to see of us. Shereene managed to swipe a duplicate of the new key for the back door before she left. Her plan was to come back late at night and get the rest of the things. Of course we never did. It was always too risky. What was left just had to be left.

It was time to close that chapter of a life of misery. That house had brought me nothing but nightmares into reality. I was now looking to the future and making my life good for a change. We settled into the new big house that we had and then began to strip down everything and decorate. It wasn't an easy job; there was a lot of rubbish to clear out and a lot of cleaning and decorating. We all pulled together and did the best we could to the best of our abilities. We had to recarpet the whole house, which cost more than eight hundred pounds and instantly cancelled out us paying the rent in advance, as it wouldn't have been fair. We had a few initial problems, which were soon ironed out. It took us about six weeks to get the house to a loveable state. It wasn't perfect and, to be honest, I preferred my comfortable old house. But this was a new beginning. I had to try.

We were all getting on really well. Shereene formed a relationship with one of the guys called Tom. They were so loved up, it was a beautiful thing. James and I were just friends, and we didn't want to get into the whole relationship thing, as it would just complicate things. Well, that's what he said. So I was cool with whatever. We all lived together and were happy for a while, until James decided that he didn't want to be just friends anymore.

All the things that happened in between are irrelevant. I don't need to disclose such personal information, but, yes, I can confirm

I was now in a new relationship. And yet again, I was thrown back into that same cycle.

James was quite jealous and controlling. He didn't want me to leave his side, always wanted my attention, and was upset if I went anywhere, as he wanted my company. But amongst all this, he was still messing around with other girls. He used to still bring other girls to the house, and then after they were gone, sleep in my room. He chose to have the bedroom downstairs so that no one would know what he was doing. He thought that every time he brought a girl in the house, I wouldn't know. But he was so wrong. Another thing I discovered with James was that every time he did it or did anything wrong that would hurt me if I knew, he became very playful and liked to mess around. That was the guilt kicking in. It was his way of saying sorry, but he just didn't know it.

During this whole time, I didn't really have time for Junior. He was fading further and further into the background and he realised it. He knew something or someone was taking my time, and he knew it wasn't him. He wasn't quiet about it either. He used to ring me and curse me off and cause arguments, just because he couldn't hear from me and because I wasn't sending him money or paying him any attention. Tom and James were what you would call stereotypical "Yardies." They and their friends were in a war with some English boys from the local area. It had always been like this, as the Eng- lish boys had maintained for years that these "yard men" had come to their country and taken away all their girls. The problem was that English boys didn't know how to look after their women, so they easily lost them to this set of men who lavished them with gifts and so-called love. I remember a few incidents where the guys I lived with and their friends were constantly getting caught up with these guys from the other gang and they were fighting. By this time I had become uneasy again and occasionally was staying at my mum's house at night time. The guys had also been experiencing strange feelings, and a lot of nights they didn't come home either, which annoyed me because there was no way I was going to stay in that house alone as Shereene and I were slowly drifting apart and she didn't stay there a lot of the time either.

Because of this situation, James told me to look for somewhere else to live, because he didn't want to live there anymore and he didn't want me to be there either. I looked around until I found an apartment a bit on the outskirts of Derby. It was just right for three of us James, Tom and I. It was clean, already decorated, perfect. James hated Shereene, and he didn't want her anywhere near the new house. I never knew what made him hate her, but as he was supposed to be my partner, it made me dis- tance myself from her also and as I mentioned before we weren't really getting on well anymore anyway. She always seemed to wind the guys up in one way or another. I paid the deposit, signed all documents, and arranged to move in on that Sunday. Finally, I was leaving this house and trying to yet again start a new life. But it wasn't going to happen so easily.

I was at my mum's all day on the Saturday before I was moving, as the guys were still staying far from the house, and I wanted to spend time with my parents. I was tired and didn't feel like I wanted to go home. But I didn't want to wake up in the morning either and hear my dad harassing me to go to church, so I pushed myself to go home. This particular night I went home from my mum's house and I felt really uneasy. Strangely enough, I didn't even change my clothes into bed clothes. I just felt strange. I remember lying on my bed and watching telly until the telly was watching me. Shereene's ex-boyfriend was in the house from London (by now, she and Tom had split up), so he and a friend were down to stay. When I got into the house, I didn't even know that Shereene had gone out clubbing and that the guys had again had a confrontation with the rival gang earlier in the evening. All I knew was that I was feeling really uneasy.

It was about four a.m. and it felt as if something was trying to wake me up. I woke up suddenly. Instantly, I looked at the telly because I was facing in that direction, and then I looked behind me. I was in so much shock. When I looked behind me, I saw Shereene's ex-boyfriend standing there with an overly large Samurai sword behind his back. It was so surreal that I couldn't believe what was going on. It was one of those moments that felt like you were still dreaming. He turned around and looked at me, and then went out of the door without saying anything. It took me a few minutes to come to my senses, as I was still in shock and trying to work out if I was dreaming or if that really just happened.

All of a sudden, a scream came from the landing. I jumped up off the bed and started tiptoeing toward the door. I was hearing some kind of noise coming from outside of my door and in the front bedroom, which was next to my room. When I opened my room door, I was met by fighting and a very drugged up young individual. There was a gang war going on in the midst of my house. I was on the top floor, so I was too high up to jump out of the window. I didn't know what to do. I slammed my door shut. My legs and arms turned into jelly. I was so scared, I was panicking. Who should I call? I was still in shock. I remember calling James, nearly crying down the phone, and I was telling him what was happening. He told me to come for them where they were. I had to wait till the fight died down. All these boys were running through my house, drugged up to their eyes, throwing pots and pans around, turning everything upside down. They even kicked the front door off the hinges.

Shereene and I had not been on good terms, because she was upsetting people in the house. So I think this was the last straw. I found out later on that she was told not to go out because of a fight that happened earlier, but she went anyway. The guys followed her back to the house, kicked the door off, and started it all there. Folks, I could be dead now, killed in my bed. My parents could have received the news the next day that whilst I was sleeping, I was murdered. But by the grace of God … I went to get the guys and they were going mad. They were ready to look for these guys and kill them. They even wanted to kill Shereene, as they understood that it was because of her that this had happened. I could have been hurt. James was not happy. He was going mad. He rang Shereene, and he was shouting at her amongst her pleading for him to believe she didn't do it on purpose. He promised her that he would go to her mum's house and bottle bomb it, if anything else happened. I had never seen him so mad before. We drove around the area a few times, but we didn't see the guys. So I dropped them back, and then I went back to the house. Approaching the house, I realised the police had closed off the bottom and half way down the road. I drove passed and around to the other side of the road and parked the car. I realised I had to do a lot of lying to get through the next thirty minutes of my life. I walked down the road toward the house, and a police officer stopped me. Again, I would have received an award for this next performance.

I started to be hysterical in asking what was going on and what had happened. I was almost shedding tears. I wanted to know what was going on. They had been through my bag and got my passport out, so they wanted me to confirm my name. The head officer came to me and explained he wanted to speak to me. He said that he had questioned Shereene about what had gone on, and she couldn't make any sense in her answer. He told me what he thought had happened and explained there was damage all over the house, doors ripped off hinges, and so on. I went along with him as if I never knew anything, and he bought it. The police left and Shereene attempted to talk to me. I wasn't interested. They could have killed her that night, and I wouldn't have cared. Because of her, I nearly lost my life. So when I heard her screaming because her ex-boyfriend was beating her up that night, I didn't feel one bit sorry for her.

Through everything that had been going on and the uneasiness that I had been feeling, if I had not found somewhere else to live, I would have been in a situation. I was planning to move into the new apartment the next day, which was Sunday. It was as with the old house that I moved out of to move into this one. If I had not been looking, I wouldn't have anywhere to go when this had happened. There was no front door; it was kicked off clean.

If my memory serves me right, I think they had to push a bicycle against it to keep it closed. Can you imagine? I really didn't want to be there when the landlord came to see there was no front door on his house. He was a drug addict and quite mental at the best of times. He wasn't the easiest person to deal with.

Morning lighted out quite quickly, as by the time I was going to bed it was around seven thirty a.m. I woke around eleven a.m. and instantly began to pack up my things and inquire where I could get a removal van to move my things out that same night. During the course of the day, the landlord came around and noticed that there was no handle on the front door. The guys told him what had happened and he was fuming. Just to pacify him, they told him they were going to fix it on Monday, as we were moving out that night but didn't want him to know that.

Seven o'clock came and we moved out as quickly as possible. Again it was one of those situations where I had to make the decision of leaving the big objects, because it would be hard to move them out, as at any time the landlord could have passed by and seen what we were doing, risking some kind of confrontation if that had happened.
The removal van had to make four trips, and I loaded up about three big black cabs full of things. Shereene was there and tried to talk to me, but I couldn't. I was still so mad at what she had done. I didn't want to hear any explanation. I was quite upset that she didn't have more bruises than the few she did, considering she could have cost me my life. It sounds horrible, but I didn't care. She hurt my feelings. That should never have hap- pened. She was careless and was only thinking about herself. So in turn I wanted revenge.

6
Holding the Blade

I realised that nothing was good when we moved in to that house and nothing good would have come out of living there. After three months, nothing but complete misery ruled and reigned there. It was time for a fresh start, time to try and move on into my future, even though I never knew what I was going to do or even what I wanted to do. All I knew was that I was moving again with wrong company and a man that I thought I loved at the time.
It took a few days to sort the house out, as you can imagine when you move, but it was comfortable and I was happy. I felt safe and at peace. I was secure.

Daily life continued to consist of me being in the house, as usual, under the rule of this man with whom I had now formed a relationship. He was controlling like my husband, and he liked to get his own way all the time. If he didn't, he would be upset with me and ignore me for days. So I always tried my best to please him and not upset him. But, of course, it didn't always work.

I had moved further away from my parents' home, and I already was a bit distant. So you can imagine now how I was nearly cut off. Again it seemed like I was in a cycle. Whilst I was with my husband, I went through the same motion of feeling distant and trapped and away from my family. Even though I did not see it at the time, and even though I was happy with this man, I did not see that it would wind up in destruction in the end. Then here I was again in a relationship with another man and he was controlling me, not wanting me to leave the house, always want- ing me by his side. The only thing left for him to do was beat me and, yet, I did not see this pattern emerging again.

There were three guys and me living in this three-bedroom apartment. Surprisingly, it wasn't that cramped. They were not there a lot of the time; it was just me and James. I didn't really mind, because it was more time to spend with him. I was happy; he made me smile all the time. He seemed so real and genuine. The only problem was that he had girls, girls, and more girls in different area codes, and he didn't care. He tried not to throw it in my face, but how could he not? I wasn't stupid. I knew everything. Some would say that what he does behind my back should not hurt me. Why would I set out to discover what I didn't know? But I couldn't help it. I couldn't accept that I had to share my man with others again, but I did. I couldn't talk to any man. If I called a man, he would create a scene. But he could do anything he wanted. He once told me that "women can't do what men do!" What a statement. I never wanted to do what men do. I just wanted him to respect me more than he did and stop sleeping around whilst being in a relationship with me. I mean, was it too much to ask?

It was the middle of January, and my brother who lived in Switzerland was getting married to a girl he met over there. When my mum said we had to go to the wedding, I thought, Wow, he is actually serious about this. I was in shock more than anything else. The day I told James, I don't think he believed me. I had to make it appear as if I didn't really want to go, but my mum said I had to because it was family.

The night before I was leaving, James said he had something really important to tell me. So he sat me down, and we were just having a normal conversation. Then he came out with it.

"A girl said she's pregnant by me, but she's lying."

I was silent; I had nothing to say. I just looked into his eyes and was stuck just looking. I couldn't get angry; I couldn't even cry. Here I was—my life looked okay and I was getting on in what I thought was happiness. Then this guy I loved came and dropped this big bombshell on me. Looking at it now, again, you can see the pattern that was emerging, but at the time I couldn't see it.

In my mind, I could not process what James had just told me. Every time I tried, my brain would reject it. It just refused to accept that this could be happening to me again. Straight away, I went to the bathroom to bathe and get ready for bed. I didn't want to talk to him, see him, or anything. I just wanted to be alone.

This new revelation changed everything. All of a sudden, my life was yet again upside down. Another man who I gave my all to, and he broke my heart. My man having a baby with someone else. Are you crazy? My brother's wedding came just at the right time to get me out of this situation for a few days, so I could clear my head and decide what to do next.

In the midst of being in a relationship with James, I was still in contact with Junior, but barely. He knew I was with someone else and was not paying him much attention, even though I con- tinued to deny it to him. I didn't want to hurt his feelings, but I didn't want to be with him anymore either. When he didn't get his own way, he would curse me off and put the phone down. He would verbally abuse me as much as he could to make himself feel better and make me feel like rubbish—and it usually worked. He had friends over here, still living in the area where I lived, and every time they saw me, they would ring him and tell him they saw me doing everything I was—and everything I wasn't— just for us to be in an argument.

It came to the point where I couldn't afford to be sending money to him anymore. The money wasn't coming in as fast as it used to again, and I really wanted to stop doing wrong and illegal things. I was due to get my university money that January. They paid me late, so I was going to get it altogether, about seven thousand pounds for the year. Stupidly, just to make him happy and be nice to me, I promised to send him two thousand pounds out of it. It came to the end of January, and because he didn't see this money, he got so mad with me. He called my friends and cursed me off to them and spoke horrible things about me. And he called my mum. I was thinking, You call my friends, you dis- respect me, and you curse me off, but why call my mum? You see, my mum and Junior always got on really well, and they liked each other. So when he called into her house, it was not a prob- lem for her. I had not let her know all that had been going on, so when he called her that time, she was none the wiser.

He started off inquiring about how she was and what she had been doing, and also by telling her what he had been doing, I know this because I was there and a witness to the fluent conversation. Then I felt the atmosphere change. My mum starting giving one-word answers, and she was saying "Okay" a lot. After about seventeen minutes of conversing, she said, "Okay, take care. Bye."

I only looked at her. I didn't want to ask what was said. I just sat quietly and stared. I knew she would tell me by herself, without prompting, if she wanted to.

"He said he is calling it a day! He said you don't listen to him, you don't respect him, and you are doing your own thing."

The look of astonishment on my face was shocking. I didn't have anything to say. I didn't want to say anything. All that was going through my head was all the years he beat me, all the weeks and months I ran up and down the motorway to see him when he was detained, the amount of money I had sent him that I didn't have, and more and more. He didn't tell my mum all that, but he decided to tell my mum that I had let him down and dissed him. I remember muttering, "I don't care." I was heartbroken. Even though I didn't want him anymore, deep down inside I still had love for him. I still wanted him to be happy in life, and I still wanted the best for him.

I was feeling quite down and depressed. I was trying to work out in my mind how he could do this. He left me. No one left me. I normally left them, when I was good and ready. I don't know if I felt half empty or half full. I was experiencing something that I had never felt before—rejection.

I knew there was always one way I could get through to Junior, no matter how much he hated me for the time being— money. If I gave him money, he would be the sweetest thing in the world. You would never believe that he left me and told every- one about it in the process.

So I opened another bank account. I had been surviving by opening bank accounts and using them to do jobs with my fraud master friends and their associates in London, as they came with big overdrafts and a credit card with £1250 on it. I called Junior one day and he didn't want to talk to me. He answered and gave me an earful before hanging up on me. I texted him and told him that I was going to give him money, but since it was over and he never wanted to speak to me again, then fine. I told him I was going out to buy a new SIM card to change my number, and he would never hear from me again. Within thirty seconds my phone rang; it was him. He relayed every possible swear word to me in patois and then asked me what I rang him for, as if he never knew.

I told him that I acquired some money and was sending him five hundred pounds. All he wanted to know was when. No "Thank you," no "Are you okay?" Just send the money quickly and then some. I didn't feel any bet- ter, but I sent it to him because I promised him and needed to keep my word.

James had been so nice to me from the time I came back from holiday for my brother's wedding, but I still had not processed the in- formation download he had given me—well, at least not properly. I just knew that he was going to be a dad again, and it was with someone who was not his girlfriend. The thing about James was that I knew him. In the short time we were together, I studied his actions and reactions. I always knew when he had done something wrong, even without him telling me, because he would always play with me and want to mess around and pay me too much attention. It was his way of making it up to me and letting me know that no matter what, it would always be me and him.

I started staying at my mum's house quite often, as I started to become sick to be around James. Sometimes I would look at him or just pass him on the landing, and I would feel physically sick. I was sick of the playing, because the more he messed around, the more I hated him, knowing he was trying to make up for wrongs he had done. So I semi-moved out back to my mum's. He used to call me often to find out where I was, because he missed me and wanted me to come home. But I couldn't. He had a car that he had bought for both of us, but he would never drive it.

One day in March, I had gone to university and Junior apparently called on the house phone, but I wasn't staying there at the time. The house phone was in my room because no one paid the bill except me, but when it rang, James decided to answer it, something he had never done before, knowing it was for me. He told Junior I was at school. When Junior called back six hours later and James answered again, it didn't go down well, even though he had left me.

I don't know why James did it; I still think he was trying to get back at me. His excuse was that the phone was in his house, so he had every right to answer it. I said no more. I wasn't going to argue with him. Junior called me on my mobile and cursed me off again, told me every bad word under the sun, and wished me dead. I mean, it seemed to go from one extreme to another with this man.

The next morning, James woke me out of my sleep with a phone call. He wanted me to come home to do something for him. I reluctantly woke up and got ready to go home, but I made a detour. Who would have known that this detour would be the worst mistake of my life? I wanted Internet banking on the last bank account that I had opened, the one where I got the money to send to Junior. I walked into the bank and asked the cashier if they could reset my Internet banking details. She said to take a seat and they would send someone to get it sorted. I sat there for five minutes, ten minutes, fifteen minutes, twenty minutes and my whole body went cold. A bad feeling went through my body, and something told me to get up and go. But, out of greed, I sat there. I felt so uneasy, so I called my friend Lawrence and told him what I went to do and how I was feeling. He told me to listen to my feelings and get out of there. It was just so strange. There seemed to be so many staff members around, yet I was sitting there so long. I was about to get up to leave when a lady came out and showed me to a teller desk where she said I would be able to sort the details out. The gentleman that was at the desk sorted all the details out for me and made me sign the papers. Then he asked me if there was anything else he could help with. I replied "no" and he began to buy time by offering me other services. I still felt uneasy, but I continued to deal with the teller.

All of a sudden, a tall man dressed in black walked into the area and sat on the chair next to me. My heart stopped beating for a split second. I was trying to look out of the corner of my eye, but I could not and would not believe what I thought I was seeing. I decided to take a full look at this person who had emerged out of the main bank and placed himself next to me. I looked to the right, gulped, and took a deep breath. It was a police officer, and I knew I was in trouble.

"Leanne Woodhouse, you are under arrest. You do not have to say anything, but anything you do say will be taken down and used as evidence against you in the court of law ..."

I was just staring at the floor. In my head, I was shocked and scared. But I was able to redial my friend who I was talking to before, so I could leave the line open for him to hear what was going on.

"Do you understand what I just said?"

I replied that I did, and then he asked me if I would come with him quietly; if I did, then he wouldn't handcuff me out of the bank. He escorted me out of the bank and to the police car. We got into the car, and he said that he would like for me to keep my phones but that I had to turn them off and not call anyone. As we were going to the police station, he was asking me some questions, which I made sure to answer carefully. I needed to remember the answers I was giving, in case they asked me again at the station. I was worried for the guys in my house.

They didn't have your regular nine-to-five job. In fact, they didn't have any job— well, anything they were doing was highly illegal and carried a large prison sentence. At that point, I just remember thinking that they were going to prison and it was my fault. They would kill me or send their family to kill me. My head instantly started to hurt me. I had to let them know what had happened, but how? They needed to get out of the house.

We reached the police station, and I was in the reception for a bit, waiting to fill out forms before I was booked. Something within me prompted me to try and text somebody. So I turned my phone on under my arm and had to text without looking at the screen. I knew that this was the last chance to get to them and alert them to what was happening. I managed to send the text and the phone number for James, so my friend could call him. I don't know how I managed to get away with it, but he was able to alert them so they would get out of the house.

Booked in and put into a cell, they promised that it would not be long till they interviewed me. But how wrong they were! At that point, they had no case against me. They did not even know why they had arrested me, and they definitely did not have any evidence. They had me locked up for thirteen hours before they interviewed me. It took them that long to collect evidence, search my house, and make a case.

I was going through pain in that cell. I cried more than you could ever imagine. I promised God that if He got me out all right that I would serve Him forever. I promised to devote my life to Him, if he just let everything be okay. When people are in desperate situations and they have tried everything, God is always the last resort. They think, Well, I have tried everything, so why not try God? That was me; I just had to believe He would come through for me.

The cell was cold and dreary. I sat on the edge of the bunk, staring up outside. I saw day turn into night. The seconds, min- utes, and hours felt like days. I couldn't sleep. I just wanted them to come and get me out. Time just seemed to have stopped.

Around ten thirty p.m., they came for me so that they could interview me. I was so relieved to get out of the cell and see people. I was a wreck by the time they wanted to interview me. They put me in the room and set the tapes to record. I had to say my name, address, date of birth, and answer the questions clearly and concisely for the purpose of the tape.

They questioned me in regards to opening eighteen bank accounts with the same bank. I couldn't lie, because I did. The only thing they said I did wrong was that I lied, because they said that when you open an account, you are asked to sign that you do not have any other accounts with the bank. I had signed and said I didn't. They couldn't charge me with money laundering or any- thing, because every account I opened was opened in my real name. When they totalled up all the money owed within a period of six months, it was more than forty-eight thousand pounds. How did I get so much money out of eighteen bank accounts? Just know that I had done it and it was illegal, as I never had any intention of paying it back.

They had been to my home and had the pleasure of telling me that I was homeless, because the landlord said he did not want me back there. They also took pleasure in telling me that they had cleared the house of things that did not even belong to me. They seized everything in the house that could move: clothes, shoes, trainers, televisions, everything. As I sat in that interview room, I just wanted the ground to open up and swallow me. I wanted them to lock me up then and there, because I knew that when they let me out, I would be dead anyway, one way or another. The guys would get me because, at this point, they were homeless.

The officers dropped me home at my mum's house, as I had no money. I didn't even have keys to get into my house. They kept my phones, my passport, everything. I remember walking into my mum's house, feeling so lost. My mum was at work, and my dad was asleep in the living room. I went to my room and cried. I ran a bath because I felt really dirty, but I just cried. I did not know what to do. They had bailed me and set a court date, which was in two months, as they needed time to continue their investigation. They took James's car, and I had nothing. I didn't know how I was going to tell him. I didn't even know how to tell him he was homeless. I had ruined everything. At this point, the fact that he had been cheating on me was insignificant. It seemed like I had really got my own back on him, even though it was not intentional.

I lay in my bed and I couldn't sleep. I didn't want to hide it from my parents, but I didn't want to tell them either. How would I tell them that I had been locked up all day and questioned about something I had done wrong yet again. The feelings that were going through me were hate for myself. I started beating myself up emotionally and blaming myself for life. I literally wanted to die. I didn't see the purpose of continuing to live. The way I saw it, if I didn't kill myself, then the people I had hurt by way of my actions would kill me. I had made myself a moving, breathing target because of stupidity and because of the kind of friends that I used to move with.

I curled up into a ball and continued to cry and have my own pity party. I reached for a bottle of painkillers because, through all the crying and thinking, I was developing a migraine. I held the bottle of pills in my hand, and as I went to pour out two to take, in a split second, it was as if someone was whispering in my ear, "End it. They won't miss you. They wouldn't even notice. At least if you are dead, you can't turn people's lives upside down anymore …" These thoughts and feelings were going through my mind and tormenting me. I didn't know what to do anymore. Every decision I had ever made always turned out to be wrong. I always seemed to get myself in some sort of trouble because of not thinking before I acted.

That split second of turmoil was soon over, and I managed to suck it up and get on with working out how to tell my parents. It came to the place that I couldn't even attempt to kill myself. As before, I didn't like pain, and to kill myself would inflict some kind of pain. So I gave that idea up.

I picked up the phone and dialed my mum's work number. It

rang twice and I hung up. Fear came over me, and I felt as if I couldn't get my words out. I took a deep breath and gave myself a power talk. I told myself to toughen up and not to be afraid, because she couldn't kill me. I tried again. Ring ring, ring ring

... "Hello, Nurse Burke speaking. How may I help you?" "Mum," I said in a soft, quiet voice.

"Leanne, what are you doing? Are you all right?"

"Y-e-ah," I sobbed.

"Leanne, what's wrong? Why are you crying?"

"M-u-u-m ..." My soft crying turned into loud groaning. "I got in trouble today. I wrote some cheques and spent some money that wasn't mine. And now they are going to take me to court. I've been at the police station all day."

"Oh, Leanne, I told you about this. And now you've put yourself in a position. What did they say? What is going to happen from here?"

I explained the day's events to my mum, but I didn't tell her all the details. I tried to keep it as minimal as possible. Obviously, I had to let her know that I was now homeless and that the police seized the majority of my things. But I couldn't tell her about the guys, as she didn't even know I was living with anyone.

The situation that I had now found myself in was so scary. I didn't know what the outcome would be. I didn't know what kind of evidence they were going to come up with. Anything was liable to happen. I had done a lot of bad things in my past, and this investigation could have led anywhere. I could have been facing prison for many years. Fear gripped me, fear of the unknown. What could I do? I never reached church so quickly. Sunday came and I was up rather early, to get ready to go into the house of the Lord. All I knew was that I had tried everything, and everything had failed me. I was on a path to destruction, and the only thing I hadn't tried in a while was God. I had left the church the first time because I felt empty. Something was missing, and I was searching for that missing piece in my life to complete me. Now I was back again, and I still hadn't found the missing piece.

The service that day was just as I remembered it being seven years before, when I was bored and clock watching to see when it would finish so I could go home. I went to meet with God in my hour of need, but I was still empty. The rush of having to be in church soon died down, and I was still searching. In the following weeks, I stayed at home and watched Christian television. Every time I turned on the television, I would hear someone speaking to my need, the way I was feeling at the time or what I was going through. I knew God was speaking to me. It was the first time in my life. I couldn't feel Him, but I knew He cared and loved me. I knew He was calling my name.

During this time, I had seen Shereene and we made up again and became friends. She had a flat for her and her son not too far from where I was living. I was still cautious of her because of the hurt she had caused me in the past but I just couldn't be upset with her and had to forgive her. I think I was just too soft.

I remember going to a church for a Christening earlier in the year and really enjoying it. I really felt like I fit in there. It was lively and the people seemed so nice. I called my friend Shereene and told her that the following Sunday we were going to church, because I was still shy and did not feel comfortable going on my own.

Sunday came and I got ready, went to pick up Shereene and her son, and we went to church in the morning. I was so overwhelmed. I felt like I was home. I was reduced to tears by the word of God, "go forth," and I asked God to come into my life. There was no big bang or fire-works. I didn't feel anything, but I believed in Him and what He did for me on the cross.

Days, weeks, and months passed, and I continued to go to this new church. But I also had to attend my mum and dad's church, because I was scared to tell them that I had found a new church to go to. One day, my mum questioned me about it and said I can't be going to two churches, that I must make up my mind. I think she expected me to say that I will stop going to the new church, but I didn't. I said, "Well, if I have to decide, then I can't go to your church anymore." I explained that I had to be where I was comfortable. She asked me if I had asked God about it, and I had, but I wasn't sure if it was my mind telling me to stay or Him. The final decision was made when I asked God on a serious note to give me a sign about where I am to go, because I didn't want to do anything that would make Him mad at me. I was at my old church at a meeting one Saturday night and a song that I had never heard before reduced me to tears, "Alpha and Omega." I didn't know why, but I felt like He was doing some- thing on the inside of me. I went home at the end of the night and went to my new church the next morning, and guess what song they sang? "Alpha and Omega." That was my confirmation right there. God was telling me that no matter where you are, as long as He resides there, it's where I should be.

I officially left my old church, and whenever anyone asked where I was, my parents said that I was now going to my new church. Some of them were happy that I was in church and not bothered, but some people took it to heart and stopped talking to me. They treated me as if I had offended them or told lies about them or something. It was as if I did something forbidden. One person wanted to know what my new church had that her church didn't have. I was ready to give her the long list, but something held my tongue. I was free, all those bad church experiences were behind me. I was still a bit cautious and I was willing to give it time to see if this was going to be the same wounding experience as I had all those years ago. I was so happy in my new surrounding that I strongly believed that God put me where I would be comfortable to worship Him. He put me where He could use me. He put me where I would be of benefit. I found God, and my life was complete. And then He gave me a new home where I fitted and could start my new life. During these times, I continued to pray about my situation, and my parents continually held me up in prayer. I realised I was gaining strength from day to day to carry on. I was able to believe in this man called Jesus. I was at peace because I had a knowing that everything was going to be okay with me.

I regularly saw the guys who I used to live with, and they kept asking me for money for their things and threatening me. All I had to do was get a glimpse of them and fear would grip me. By this time, I had moved out of my mum's house again to a new apartment nearby. I had been away from home for so many years that there was no way I could live back there permanently. I had to get out as soon as I could. I was used to my own way and used to not having to answer to anyone, having my own freedom. I know my mum really wanted me to be near her, but I just couldn't. I say I couldn't, but I was away for one month and had to move back home again. I wasn't managing because, yet again, money wasn't really coming in as fast as it used to, and I wasn't working at the time. I had bills and rent to pay. I couldn't start asking my mum to sub me every month; it wouldn't have been fair. So I had to give up and initially decide to go back home for six months, until I got myself back together and back on my feet.

My mum and dad were glad to have me back under their roof so they could monitor what I was getting into. I was trying to sort out James's car, which the police had taken from me and were not willing to give back. It was in my name and, therefore, they were saying I could have bought the car with money from my bank account, which was totally untrue. It wasn't even mine really; it was just registered to me. In a hope of getting it back, I put the car in a friend's name so he could claim it back and then give it to me to give back to James. What a big mistake! I was due to go to the police station in May to sign some paperwork, and I nearly collapsed when the officer in charge of the case told me the owner had been in for the car and had taken it back. The so-called fiend who I trusted had the car and didn't tell me. Not only did he keep it from me, but he had sold it. The room grew dark around me as I tried to process what had happened. I called James as soon as I got out of the police station to tell him what had happened with the car, and he rang the friend who had sold it. A little later in the day, I received a phone call from James.

"He said you knew about him having the car and that you told him to sell it, and he gave you half the money ..."

Again, I really could not process what I had just been told. This man had made up this lie and delivered it to the people who already wanted to kill me so they would kill me quicker. I started to cry. I was in pain. How could he have done this to me? I had no leg to stand on. James didn't have to believe me. And I am sure that at times he really didn't want to; but he did. He knew my character and knew I would never do anything like that to anyone, let alone him. I loved him too much. Could things get any worse? I was stressed out with this big court case, and now people were swindling me and telling lies on top of it. I just knew that, in the end, everything was going to be okay. I had a feeling deep down in my soul. I had to believe. I didn't know how or when, but I knew I was coming out.

I was in Footlocker one day with my friends, and James and the guys I used to live with walked in. I saw them and my heart skipped beats. I was cornered; I didn't know what to do. I was scared for my life, and no one could help. James didn't want to talk to me, but his brother came over to me. He wanted to know how they could be homeless and have nothing left because of me, and yet I was in Footlocker buying trainers with my friends. He said that I wouldn't leave that shop that day unless I bought some- thing for them all. They were mad, and I felt in my bones that they would have beaten me up in the shop. I was scared for my life. After arguing with them, saying that I had no money, I could see that I was not getting out of there. So I agreed. They picked up trainers and I paid for them. About two hundred fifty pounds was spent. I was prepared to do anything to get out of the shop. I left the shop with no hesitation and went straight home. About half an hour after the confrontation, James called me. He said he wanted to see me later that day. I agreed at first, but then quickly tried and get out of it by saying I was going to Nottingham. He was adamant that he wanted to see me before I went, so again I agreed. Do you really think I would have gone to meet him? I feared that if I did, it would have been the end of me. I turned my phone off and stayed indoors. The next day, he called and asked me why I was messing around with him. He said that I ruined his life, and I should be grateful that he was still talking to me. This was his way of telling me that he was no longer upset with me and was willing to remain friends. After all he put me through, he wanted to be back in my life... There was just no way.

I had been to court twice since I got arrested, and each time the case was adjourned. So I still didn't know if I was coming or going. My solicitor had assured me that if, when I went the next time, they didn't have any evidence, then the case would have to be thrown out because it was wasting people's time. My next court date was in November 2006, and it was then June. I didn't know what I was going to do to occupy my time until November. I felt useless and I was getting lazy, getting up late every day and doing nothing from day to day. There had to be something more to life than the way I was living it. I was getting the notion that the point of living was nonexistent.

Around that time, I had become quite dependent on God. I had formed a relationship with Him in a way that, when I was lonely, I would talk to him. When I needed comfort, I believed He would give it to me. Sometimes I would hear scriptures from the Bible as if they were being read to me. These words were comforting me and giving me a hope for the future.

This time in my life was quite confusing. I didn't know where I was supposed to be. But one thing I did know was that I felt like I was being called into a higher calling. I felt as if I was being called to a place I had never been before, into a new experience.

7
I Am the Way

After long contemplation, I decided that I was going to look for a job, because I really couldn't sit at home doing nothing. I applied to an agency and was positioned within the local water board. It was a customer service position working in their financial returns (refunds) department. It was a job. At that point, I didn't care if I enjoyed it or not. It was occupying my time and giving me money. The bonus on top of it was that I actually did enjoy it.

It wasn't long before I began to understand the operations of the job. There was a lot of fraud going on within the company, and, at the time, it was something that I really tried not to get caught up in. For the work I was doing, it just didn't seem like I was being paid my worth. The thoughts of being underpaid began to cross my mind more often. I fought them off for a few weeks until, out of desperation, I tried cheating the company. I got dragged into the system; I was now doing as others did. You may be thinking, But I thought she was a Christian and was serving God. Well, my reply to that is, “Even Christians fall.” I got myself in a situation that I had tried to resist and failed. I did it once, and it was so easy that doing it again was no sweat for me—until I became addicted to doing it. After a few months of doing it, I became conscious of what I was really doing, and fear began to grip me. I needed to stop one way or another, but how? On my own, I couldn’t do it.

I was in a constant battle, wanting to do right, but evil would always present itself. My court case was coming up again, and it had seemed as if I hadn’t even learned my lesson. Here I was doing more rubbish to get myself into more trouble. It was as if I didn’t care about my future or something.

My court date was drawing nearer, and my lawyer called me into the office. He said that he didn’t think it was really necessary for me to come to court that day, because he didn’t believe that the bank would show up again and that they would request to postpone again. It was great news for me, because I was still believing that God would do a miracle on my behalf. The day eventually arrived, and the phone call that I wanted to hear all day came around two o’clock p.m.

“Miss Woodhouse, the case has been thrown out. It’s great news and you can return to regular living with no worries.”

My parents were over the moon to hear that. I remember my mum saying, “Thank God, just praise Him …”

Yes! The case was over and I wasn’t going to prison. The police got in touch with me to release my things, and I was able to get on with my life again as normal. But it wasn't normal, was it? I was still battling with the current job position I had. I was being tempted day in and day out, tempted to do things that were ungodly and criminal.

Around this time, some jobs came up in a different department where I wouldn't have this head-on temptation. So I decided to apply. Fortunately, I got the job and was relieved to be out of the environment that had birthed this obsession of deceit in me. New job, new people, new job description—great! But I wasn't enjoying it as much as my old job. The people weren't great, and I just felt out of place. When I saw a colleague taking a picture of customer credit card details, I realised I had to get out of there. I was surrounded by people who were swindling this company for anything they could get. I applied for a new job outside of the company and managed to get it. I was so grateful. I realised that it had started off badly for me in the water company, and I needed to get out whilst I could still swim.

I needed a change of atmosphere. I wanted to be good and live an honest life, but I still felt an inner battle that made me believe it wasn't possible. I had some friends who used to say I only went to church because I was in trouble and it wouldn't last long. They thought that I would be back in the clubs, running up and down like a headless chicken again soon. Well, they are still waiting to see it happen after nearly three years. And they will never see it. I am far from perfect, and maybe when I first went back to church it was because I had exhausted every other measure, but I am still here, still walking by faith and not by sight.

I handed my notice in one week before I was due to start my new job with a major electricity and gas provider, about twenty- five miles out of my hometown. I was excited, as this would be a new challenge, and I was running away from what could have been the next major problem in my life.

They accepted my resignation, and I prepared myself to commute daily to my new, exciting position.

Again I felt like I was starting a new section of my life. Maybe this move would do me good, and I was really positive about what was to come. All of my life, I just wanted to be happy and never quite made it, because I kept making the wrong decisions all the time. They say that the choices you make form your future. I did a lot of wrong things back in the days, and every major thing I did has caught up with me, with justice being served in one way or another.

I was so excited and pumped up with energy on starting this new job, but in the back of my mind, I was wondering how long this motivation would last. How long would I be able to continue waking up extra early every day to commute twenty-five miles per day, sometimes in heavy traffic lasting as long as two and a half hours?

I was on a high. I had slowly made friends with a few people at church; however, because I was shy, I didn't talk to them that much. I wanted to express myself, but I was too concerned at the time with getting used to my new environment.

The more I attended church, the more I started to get involved in activities and interact with people more. One of the girls at church sent me some information about a singles camp that some of them were attending, and she asked me if I wanted to go. I thought it was a good chance to get to know them better and learn a different way of life. After all, the kind of friends I used to have were in my past. I had taken a new road, and I had new friends to show for it. It was at this time in my life that things started to look up. I was consumed with God and His love for me. I was studying the Bible and praying earnestly. I suppose sometimes that, in the beginning, things seem easy, but they did eventually get harder.

I believed in God because He gave me hope. I believed in Him and I was so grateful to Him, because in my hour of need He delivered me. He kept me, He sheltered and comforted me, and He gave me strength to carry on. God had done so much for me, and I wasn't going to turn my back on Him once everything was all right. In the past, I had made Him so many promises to live right and for God if He would let certain things happen. But when those things happened, I didn't honour my promise. This was not going to be another one of those times. This time, I was not going to break my word.

At times it was hard. I had my old friends who were always trying to entice me and draw me back to where I was in bondage, but I was always given the added strength to carry on. I am not going to lie and say that I wasn't sometime tempted, because I was. Sometimes I used to wonder what was going on in the circle I had left. I used to wonder what people were getting into and what things had kicked off at that point, but I had the grace bestowed upon me to keep focused.

Do you remember James? My now ex-boyfriend whom I loved with all my heart? Well, I still did. Junior was clearly out of the picture. I didn't even remember anything about him, unless someone mentioned his name. And I wasn't around anybody to mention his name, so I was safe. But James had a hold over me that even witchcraft couldn't put on me. I loved him more than you could think or imagine. There was nothing too good for him. Even though I had given up that kind of living, my feelings for him didn't leave overnight. I continued to battle with the feelings for a good future. Sometimes I used to cry because I didn't want to love him anymore. It was a distraction to have him on my mind and to be thinking about the things we used to do together. I would close my eyes and hear his voice. I would see his face. The soul ties that had been created with him were so strong that even my prayers were not breaking through concerning the issue. The more I wanted to forget him, the more he would ring me or I would see him around. I contemplated leaving Derby a few times, just because I didn't want to do anything wrong. I didn't want to end up in a compromising situation with this guy that I was still in love with and who still loved me.

As time went on, I continued to seek God and move my mind on to good things and away from evil and James. It was hard, but I knew one day I would get a release. It affected me to the point where I was often thrown into bouts of depression. I had suffered from depression since about age sixteen, around the time I started having relationships. It never left me; it just had its times when it would affect me and times when I would be okay. Those times when nothing was going right and the voices were in my head telling me to end it all—it was commonplace for me to hear these things when I felt down and unloved.

Even though I was in church, no matter how lovely the peo- ple were, I sometimes went home and felt unloved because of whatever situation I was going through. I could never talk to my mum, because I was always scared she would judge me. She knew how she brought me up, so in her opinion, I shouldn't have been carrying on with the rubbish that I was going on with. Even now whilst I am writing this book, I am wondering how she is going to react or feel when this book hits the shelves and she buys a copy. What will be running through her mind, knowing her daughter was involved in so much badness with people who were totally wrong for me? All I know is that was then, and this is now. I am a brand new creation.

The time was approaching for the singles camp that I was going on with a few of the guys and girls from my church. To be honest, I was quite fearful of going. Remember, I was shy and didn't really know these people. Here I was going all the way to Norfolk with them for a long weekend for a singles camp. Norfolk was about 4 hours drive from Derby, so it was more than a stone throw away. It sounds crazy. What was I doing? Where was I really going? Who told me to pick up myself to go anywhere?

Work was going quite well. Every day I was so energised and had a passion to be there. When I was working there, it was then that my prayer life was at its strongest. Whilst I was driving down the motorway daily, I used to bring down the roof, praying and singing to my God. He used to meet with me on the way to work. We would commune. I felt His presence so profoundly. Prayer was not a chore for me during this season of my life. I felt at ease; it was so easy for me to get into prayer. At lunch times, I would also spend my hour in the car praying. I felt such a passion, it was as if my life depended on it. This is what I was longing for; the void in my life that I had harboured for so many years was filled. Never in the history of me going to church from when I was a child have I ever experienced what I was experiencing during this time. If you are not a Christian or you don't know if you believe in God or not, just ask Him to help you make up your mind. Don't take my word for it; ask God for signs to enable you to believe. That's all I am saying about that.
The feelings I had once held for James were fading fast. He was becoming a distant memory and I didn't care. I was happy and nothing else mattered.

I had been in contact with the police station, as my case was over and they had to return all the things that they had seized. It had been more than a year, and I was not really in need of any- thing again. But it was just great to have them back, and the boys (James and Tom) would have been glad to get their things back. I arranged a day to go down to the station to get everything back. I didn't realise how much stuff I had; after so long it had slipped my mind. It took my big car, my mum's car, and a taxi to retrieve everything from the police station. But the majority of the things were more than a hundred boxed pairs of trainers, which belonged to James. We won't even venture into the reasons why he had so much footwear. But all I will say is he hasn't changed; he is obsessed and needs counselling, or maybe prayer.

Finally, I was able to close that chapter of my life. I had all my belongings back and I was able to return the boys' things to them. Of course, they were glad to get them back. But what I hadn't bought back for them over the course of the year, they had bought back for themselves. So it meant they had a lot of duplicated clothes and accessories. I felt at ease knowing that they had nothing to hold against me. I had been stupid, and they were caught up in the crossfire. But now I was able to make peace, because they got back everything that had been taken from them. Well, James didn't get the car back, but I sought his forgiveness and he gave it to me.

Seeing James again after so long and after I had pushed him out of my mind was quite emotional. He looked well and still had the twinkle in his eye when he saw me. Seeing him again reminded me why I fell in love with him in the first place. He was my heartbeat, and no matter who he was with at the time, he knew and I knew he still loved me. It was just the wrong time for old fires to be rekindled. Everything was going so well in my life that I really didn't want anything messing up. We had a brief conversation and I left quickly.

While driving down the road, looking in my rear-view mirror, I saw the distant image of who was once the love of my life, the man I would have done anything for, the man who I loved more than my husband. He was becoming a smaller and smaller image, until I couldn't see him anymore, the same way he had become in my real life.

It was a few days until I was embarking on my long weekend in Great Yarmouth, Norfolk, and I was actually quite excited. I felt free and had no burdens weighing me down. I was excited because I didn't know what to expect. I was hoping and praying that it was going to be a great weekend. One way or another, I was going to get around my shyness and enjoy myself.

My long weekend started on a Thursday at the end of April 2007. I finished work at five o'clock p.m. and took the long drive home to Derby through all the traffic. It was going to be a great weekend, I was beginning to embrace the fact that I had the opportunity to get to know these people that I was going away with and I was really looking forward to it. Friday soon came, and I was packing my final clothes and items to get ready to go to our meeting point, from which we would leave together. Alto- gether, there were seven of us who went from Derby. We travelled together in two separate cars.

I am laughing now as I am writing this, as it took us more than seven hours to get to Norfolk, a trip that normally takes only four hours. This was because men always think they are better than women at everything. One of the guys claimed he knew the way, and we spent three hours driving around the A47 in the wrong direction, until we decided to turn around and try to find the route again. I was going to say it was before the Sat Nav invention, but it wasn't; we just didn't have one. We finally reached our destination and everything was fine. We reached safely and charged up to get our joke and our praise on. It was a new experience to me, as I had never been to a singles camp before. I wasn't expecting to form one relationship, but instead making many new friends along the way.

When I first got there, I didn't speak much because I was still shy at that point. But I tried to settle in as much as I could and get along with everyone who was going to be within my sur- roundings for the next three days.

I don't want to bore you with every little detail of the camp, but I can say I left there forming a lot of new friendships—and I still have those friendships today. It was an experience that I will never forget and never regret. I learned so much in that one weekend than I have learned in one year. I was able to come out of my shell a bit more, the cocoon that surrounded me was slowly disappearing but I was still a long way off. God was really showing Himself strong in my life and moving on my behalf. Through prophecy, He reminded me that He had remembered me and was carrying me all the way.

We reached home late Monday evening, and I had to prepare myself for work the next day. After such a wonderful weekend, I didn't even want to come home so soon. I could have stayed in that atmosphere longer. Work was not where I wanted to be. I now knew there was something greater than a nine-to-five job every day. Well, maybe not for everyone, but there was some- thing greater for me. I didn't feel like I was fulfilling my purpose doing this job, working as a slave, as it were. Deep down inside, I wanted to work for myself to get full satisfaction. I wanted to help people. There were so many dying in the world. I knew it wasn't about me anymore.

Another reason for the strain was that, even though I was earning a large amount of money on a monthly basis, it was going out on a large scale in commuting costs. I was paying more than three hundred pounds per month in petrol to go and come from work each day. It wasn't feasible. I would have rather take a pay cut and find a job nearer home than to pump it into petrol each month.

I had a meeting with my manager at work. I explained to her how I was feeling and that I felt there had to be something else for me and that my position there wasn't it. She agreed with me in the way that you would expect, but what she said next shocked me.

"It will be a shame to lose you, but if you feel like you have to do this, then we will support you. Also, to give you enough time to find another job, we will pay you for two months, full pay."

Full pay! I still can't believe it. How many jobs that you resign from will tell you that? Even if they sack you, they don't do that. It's called divine favour. Of course, I left there at the end of May 2007 and decided that I was going to explore a bit and see which direction life would lead me in. I wasn't in a rush to find a job, as I was covered for two months, so I just chilled and waited to see what was going to happen.

I wanted and needed time to explore me—well, explore the new me. I knew the old Leanne who did all the bad things, who lied and cheated, but now I wanted to know who Leanne was with this man called Jesus living on the inside. My life had been changed, but everything had gone so fast that I didn't have time to stop, slow down, and get to know me—well, until time was made for me.

8
Wilderness

During the time that I had off from work, I was able to develop a community youth project that I was working on called Kingdom Advancement more and put some kind of structure in place. Here I had a passion placed within me to help the youth culture of today. I had a great committee team behind me who were able to catch the vision. The ideas were overflowing, and we were making headway. Every meeting we had was progres- sive, and we could see the effect of our presence and what we were doing was going to make in the community. But there were issues. I was heading everything to the point where I wanted to incorporate others into leadership, so if I was ever unable to attend or had to step down, others could take over. I decided to establish various leadership and departmental roles for each committee member to be responsible for, which would make the load easier. It was the feasible thing to do. No man is an island. No one person has got it all together and knows everything. If a leader is unable to delegate and let the help get on with what you have tasked them to do, without worrying about it, then he or she is not a leader.

Kingdom Advancement was birthed out of a passion for me to be transparent. I had been through so much, and my faith in God enabled me to conquer it all. I felt as if God was encouraging me to get out there and tell my story. And in the midst of telling my story, help people who were going through what I had been through, by letting them know if I could overcome, then so could they. I didn't know how I was going to do it, but I knew this was the initial basis from which I was supposed to start.

Church was becoming more and more of a passion for me. As time went on, I was opening up and the shyness seemed to drop from me. The first time they asked me to sing, it was as if I was the boldest person in the world. For those few minutes, nothing else mattered apart from singing my love song to Jesus. Singing was something that I always did, but when my life went downhill, I stopped doing it. Singing always used to encourage me, but I had reached a place where it couldn't work for me anymore. So I stopped. Here I was in front of many people singing, "Because of who you are, I give you glory." It was the first song I ever sang in my church. That night, I hit some notes I never knew I had in me. I went deep into worship and experienced God on a different level. I didn't see the faces of the congregation, because by the time I got to the fourth word, my eyes were closed in reverence to the God I was sending up praises to. It was an awesome experience; I will never forget it. It was the first time I was singing like this in years. I still had it, but it was better than ever. Singing instantly became a passion of mine again, and within my heart I decided that one day I wanted to put out an album. I wanted to write songs to God in worship and adoration. I am not a songwriter, but all things are possible with God. I haven't accomplished this yet, but I have said it and it is going to happen all in the fullness of time.

That day was the first day of the rest of my life. I began to experience visions and dreams, revelations about decisions that I needed to make and directions that I needed to go in. There was so much I didn't know about God, so much for me to explore and get into. The more I found out about Him, the more I wanted to know about Him. It was endless. There was a song that said, "I keep falling in love with him over and over and over and over again ..." That was it. The more I knew about Him, the more I loved and appreciated Him dying on the cross for me thousands of years ago. I was asked to join the Praise and Worship team at my church and the choir. It was an overwhelming experience, because it was as if overnight my positioning in life and ministry was changing. Here I was a girl who had been through the mill. I came to Jesus because I was desperate. I stayed with Jesus because He was more than faithful. He supported me when I was down and out. He never let me down, and now I was appointed to lead His people into worship. I didn't take this lightly. The position required a certain lifestyle that I endeavoured to live each day. You couldn't be living the life I used to live and be leading people into worship. I had to live worship, and worship is a lifestyle. You know you can get those people who are only saved on a Sunday, but Monday through Saturday they are the hottest sinners on the block. Well, that couldn't be me. I needed to be pure and holy. Nobody is perfect, least of all me, but I had to strive to be like Jesus seven days a week, twenty-four hours a day. I had a responsibility, and I didn't want to fail.

It had been an awesome year so far, and it was coming up to the annual Midlands Lighthouse Conference at my church. I was so excited. I didn't know what to expect, but I knew it was going to be great. It was a time when we had speakers and preachers come in and minister God's word to us; it was an awesome experience.

Just before the conference, I applied for a job with a major telephone provider and was appointed. The hours were strange as they were anything between 7:00 am and 12:00 midnight, and I was not really used to flexible shifts. But I decided that I was going to try, after all, I needed a job. I was there for three weeks. I managed to get through the training, as it was the normal nine- to-five day. It wasn't until the shifts started and I was sometimes leaving work at midnight that I realised that I couldn't manage this lifestyle. I tried to stick it out for as long as possible, but I couldn't. Instantly, I was scouting around for other jobs. I applied for jobs as far as Birmingham which was about fifty miles away from my home just to get out of where I was. Conference was the following week, and I had the worst shifts ever. According to the shifts I had, I was going to miss the majority of the conference. I tried to swap shifts, but no one would. I felt low within me, but one thing I knew was that I was not missing the conference for anything, especially a job I hated.

I had to make a crucial decision—stay or leave. Well, I handed in my notice and I left at the end of that week. I had not been able to secure another job yet, but I didn't care. I wanted out. I wanted to be able to go into God's house and worship Him. I didn't want to be at work wondering what was happening and what I was missing.

Conference was a blast. I was so blessed. I received the word of the Lord into my life in such a mighty way.

The Lord sent His word to remind me that He had not forgotten me and that He had favoured me. He was reassuring me that everything was going to be okay, that I just had to trust Him.

About two weeks after the conference and intense job searching, I was appointed at a major logistics company as an accounts administrator.

Again it was a new challenge. I didn't know what to expect, but I knew God would direct my path. I enjoyed the new job, and I made friends quickly with quite a few people. Over the prior few weeks, I had been feeling the gumption to start my own business. I have always been interested in event management and was always organising things for people for free. So I decided that I wanted to make a business out of it. I searched the Internet to see what courses were offered so I could qualify to follow my dreams. I researched setting up businesses and got all the information I needed to proceed. Setting up a business is not easy, but this is where I started.

Everything was going well. All aspects of my life were fruit- ful, and my faith was growing from strength to strength. But somewhere deep down inside, there was a feeling that was eating me away. The depression that I had suffered with for years was there lingering. That deep depression that took me into bouts of madness sometimes was still within. Between September of 2007 to December 2007, I went through a dramatic change. I felt so down; it was as if I really wanted to give up on life. Nothing was making sense to me. I had everything, my life was on track, but I was depressed.

Slowly but surely, I became less and less active in church and in my private activities. I had to withdraw from praise and wor- ship and the choir because I was not at ease. I was going through something that did not enable me to stand in front of a congregation on a Sunday and lead them into worship. I couldn't worship personally, so how was I going to lead others into worship?

My prayer life went downhill. Reading the Bible became a struggle and soon something of the past. I was at the point where I didn't even want to be at church anymore. My whole life felt and looked like it was a mess. It wasn't something that was blatantly obvious to people by looking at me because I was still a very private person, and unless I said that things were wrong they never knew. Of course I never said things were wrong. I had spiralling debt problems and not enough money coming in to cover them. I was earning so much money, but still spending on top. So paying old debts was a problem. You see, I was what the modern world would call a shopaholic. Even if I didn't need something, if I would never use it, as long as I had money or a credit card to charge it to, then it would be going home with me. Even today, I find some things in my house and try to remember why I bought it, because it is worthless to me. I can't figure out what would have possessed me to purchase it in the first place. I was at an all-time low. I felt like God had left me; I couldn't feel Him, I couldn't hear Him. The passion I once had for God and the things of God was gone. I didn't know what was happening to me. I was in turmoil. I was in a dark place; my mind was telling me it was time to move on. After all those years and people telling me God was the way, and I chose that way, but ended up at a brick wall. What was the point? Who was I kidding? Church obviously wasn't for me!

I started going to church less and less. I cut out Bible studies and prayer meetings. That was it. My interest was fading, but what was now filling this void that I created? My friends of old. They had been slowly seeping back into my life. I sometimes missed the life they were living and wanted it back. Just to be able to chill with them and have a laugh every now and then was all I wanted. At that point I was at church but still breaking through my shyness, so didn't really have anyone to call my bona fide friend yet. I started going around to their houses just to chat until, after a while, I got caught back up in the same old rubbish and conversations. I had been warned beforehand that this would try and happen to me. I heard a word in my spirit a few weeks before my world came crashing down. The Lord said:

"Stand fast therefore in the liberty wherewith Christ hath made us free, and be not entangled again with the yoke of bond- age." Galatians 5:1 (*King James Version*)

I heard what he was saying and I understood completely, but my feelings and my soulish being were ruling me. I was searching for something once again, and the outside world was talking to me at the time. They caught my attention, and I felt it was a place that I needed to be. I could no longer feel this God that I had grown so close to. All of a sudden, I was in the middle of a wilderness and I felt that I was alone.
On the other side, I was going through the same wilderness experience at work. These people had employed me, but didn't have any work for me to do. They were paying me for doing nothing. Sometimes I would be so bored sitting at my desk that I would fall asleep. One day that particularly stands out was when they had the air conditioning on. I mean, it was the middle of winter and they had air con on. It was about eleven a.m. and I had finished any work I would have had thirty minutes after my shift started. So you can imagine how little there was for me to do. I felt my head drop and, all of a sudden, I woke up. I was sleeping on the job! Yes, ladies and gents, people would have thought I wasn't getting

enough sleep. But, no, it was because I was bored.

I was getting so frustrated and spent my last three months there developing my business and doing things for Kingdom Advancement. Even though I was doing something constructive with their time that would benefit me in the end, I really found it was pointless and could not justify waking up early and driving out to the airport five days a week to do what I could do at home. Yes, I know I was getting paid for it, but I wasn't happy. In fact, I was far from happy.

Christmas 2007 was average for me. Really, I was just about hanging onto my faith. And, yes, I was still going to church, but all that was fading away. I had to make some crucial decisions. I had to try and work out where my life was heading. The work thing had to go. Again I found myself job hunting, looking for my next challenge of the new year. Christmas went so quickly and the new year was ushered in. My feelings didn't change; I managed to make it through the holiday season still in my right mind, but still empty. So many thoughts and feelings were going through my head, not knowing which way to turn, who I could trust, if I was now alone, or if God was with me.

I remember going home one day from work and my mum said that someone called the house for me from Jamaica. I didn't understand, but as soon as I heard the name of the person, I realised it was Junior trying to make contact. I thanked God that I wasn't there at the time; I don't think I could have made it through the day. My past had come back to haunt me. Why was he doing this? It had been more than a year, and I was getting on with my life. Why did he feel as if he had to start the new year off by reminding me of his presence? Another stress to add to my mind. I didn't really need it. Even though I had forgotten about him, in the back of my mind I was always fearful, because he promised that he would kill me. I was always scared that he would get back to this country and hurt me or my family in some way. So whenever he called into my parents' house, I was reas- sured he was still alive and that one day we might meet again.

It was a cold winter's morning, about the second week in January 2008, and I woke up to get ready for work. I sat on the edge of my bed, wanting to move but I couldn't. I broke down into tears. I really couldn't do this anymore. What was happen- ing to my life? Where was I heading? I felt like I had come to the end of the road. From that day on, I didn't go back to my job. I left because I couldn't bear going there every day and doing nothing. Instantly, everything caved in all around me—my business, my projects—I was empty and felt as if I was having a breakdown.

Instantly I dropped everything: Kingdom Advancement, Dayz 4 u, which was my event management company that I was setting up, work, and church. I needed a break before I got a break mentally. I was overwhelmed. So much was on my mind, and I couldn't see a way out.

The thing I feared the most, which was to fall back in to the state that I was in, finally occurred. I started to knock around with my old friends again, until I was going clubbing again. Don't get me wrong I wasn't standing on a street corner with them whilst they were selling drugs, but I was in their company which was bad enough. They were a bad influence from the beginning and because I didn't know what I wanted out of life, because I didn't know where I was heading I slipped back into what I thought was a comfortable place. James also came back into the picture. He was always on the sidelines ready to pounce at any given chance, and he didn't have to wait long. I remember an old friend called Dave once said to me that he was waiting to see me come back,

that he knew I couldn't ever stick at the church thing for long.
I stood there and stared at Dave. What did he mean? Who was I? What kind of role model had I become? I was professing Christ the year before, saying God is love and all that. I was liv- ing right so that my life could be a testimony to the world, but all that time my so-called friends were betting how long it would be until I moved on and came back to them. What had I become?

Had I used God to my advantage again and given up on Him when I felt alone? The comment that guy made knocked me for six. I had backslidden and everyone knew it. I was a failure and everyone reminded me of it. I started beating myself up verbally, because yet again I had failed God and myself. I was scarred by past issues and never ever dealt with them. I buried them without facing the fears, and now when everything seemed to be crashing around me, they presented themselves before me again.

If you are following this journey with me in sequence, you will remember that a few chapters ago, which equates to two years ago, I was working for the water board and some fraudulent activity went on. Well, it had been more than two years and I had taken myself out of the equation, as I didn't want to be a part of that life anymore. Anyway, it was about ten thirty a.m. on a cold Tuesday morning in February 2008. There was a heavy knocking at my front door. I was in my bed. I jumped up quickly and ran to the front of the house to look out of the window.

I saw two police officers outside, a man and a lady. Instantly, my mind was turning over. What was going on now? Why were they here? I got my dressing gown on and ran downstairs to open the door because my mum was sleeping, and I didn't want them to wake her up.

"Leanne Burke?" *(shortly after Junior got deported, I changed my name back to my maiden name by deed poll)*.

"Yes," I replied.

"We are here because we need to question you about an inci- dent that took place in 2006 when you worked at the water board."

"Um ... okay. I need to get dressed, and then I will come with you."

The lady officer came upstairs with me and she said she would wait outside my door until I got dressed. I was feeling so weak; I couldn't believe what was happening to me.

I was taken to the police station and they went through the formalities. I was placed in a cell for what felt like hours. Well, it was hours. That was about eleven in the morning, and they didn't question me until after six o'clock p.m. I felt like I was going out of my mind sitting there. I didn't want to lie down and sleep, because you just don't know what kind of people had been lying there. I didn't want to use the toilet, because I am the kind of person who scorns public toilets. I didn't want to eat their food, because you don't know what's in it. All I could do is sit and wait till they were ready for me.

I watched the day turn into night. Every second, every hour, all I could do was look at the powder green walls and read the adverts that were placed there by crime stoppers. I remember talking to God a bit. I was talking to Him about how I got here and acknowledging the fact that this thing that happened so long ago still caught up with me. I didn't know what was going to happen, but I just wanted it to be over. I prayed a prayer of faith and encouragement and left the rest to God.

They came to interview me around six p.m., and it was quite straightforward and an easy process. I didn't get a lawyer initially, because I thought it would speed up the process. But it didn't. I didn't have anything to hide. I wasn't prepared to lie. I admitted everything they said, if I had done it. I just wanted to be out of that place and home. They dealt with the matter as quickly as they could so that I could go home. In the end, they had fifteen charges against me, but actually charged me only for three. That in itself was a miracle. I was released on bail and the officers arranged for someone to take me home. As bad as the situation was, the officers were nice to me. They never treated me horribly because of the position I was in.

I walked into the house, and my mum and dad were waiting for me. They wanted to know what had happened and what was going to happen next. They did not have any idea why I was arrested, so I told them some, but not the entire story. At that point, I had decided within myself that they only needed to know the basics for prayer purposes. But I really didn't want them to worry. I know it sounds weird saying that but, over the years, I realised that I had put them through so much. I thought it was over. This came out of the woodwork and would shake anybody up. I just wanted them to have less to worry over. Obviously, they still worried a lot, so it didn't really make much difference.

I tried to get back to normal everyday life and carry on with things until my court date came along. I had a lot of contemplating to do about my actions in the past, which were now affecting my future. I also had a lot of speaking to God to do. I turned my back on Him, and here I was again in a situation that only He could bring me out of. I know He forgave me for all I had done wrong during the few months that I was on holiday from Him. I felt at peace. I wasn't worried about the situation, because I believed that whatever was to happen would be His will. I knew that God had planned the best for me, even if it didn't look good in my eyes. He knew what He was doing.

During the following month up until the trial, I continued to look for a job. But I was always worrying about what was going to happen to me. Even though I prophesied that I knew God would bring me through, sometimes it felt hard, because what I was seeing with my natural eyes said the opposite. No jobs that I was interested in came up, so I was just at home a lot of the time and trying to plan my business out. I remember the first Sunday I went to church, I had a good week and couldn't wait to be in the sanctuary. My pastor was preaching and, at the end, he said he wanted to pray specifically for those suffering from depression. Tears instantly filled my eyes. On and off for years I had been suffering from this malfunction. The past couple months of my life were consumed with depression, and I just wanted to be healed. My God, every word he prayed when he got to me went right through me. I felt the words as they penetrated something in my life. Something was happening; there was an instant change. I began to cry and couldn't stop. I was crying for at least half an hour, even when I went back to my seat. You see, I wasn't sad; there was a release going on within me that could only be completed by way of the tears that were flowing from within. I was continuing to pray for my situation and believing God for a miracle. I knew that whatever the outcome, I would be able to bear it by His strength. But I just held on to the fact that the worst wouldn't happen.

I went to the first court hearing and they just asked me to confirm my name, age, address, and plea which of course was guilty.

Then they gave me a date to come back for the actual trial.

I was getting back into church activities and life, and I realised that since the prayer that was prayed over me in conjunction with the spirit of depression, I never felt the same again. That release that I experienced was so profound that I knew something had broken within me.

Time went quite quickly between the first hearing and the second. It was two days before my hearing on the second of April, and something moved within me to send a text out to everyone I knew to pray with me. I didn't release the details, but I explained that I was going through a hard time and I needed their prayers because a decision had to be made concerning my future, and I needed it to be within God's will. I got responses and replies as people joined with me in prayer. Some might say it wasn't enough, but it was. I was never going to be prepared for what was about to happen to me.

The court day arrived and I woke up positive, adamant that I was coming home from court that day free as a bird. My friend from church came with me because she didn't want me to go on my own. I was on top of the world; I felt like nothing could knock me down. I was making plans for the rest of the day and was generally quite happy. I had to wait about an hour before I went in, but my lawyer assured me the worst that could have happened for this charge was community service. Finally, it was my turn. I walked into the courtroom and sat behind a glass wall. We went through the formalities and then the magistrate asked me a sequence of ques- tions pertaining to the case and my actions. I answered them the best way and only way I knew how to. I didn't lie. I was a hundred percent truthful. The time came for the judge to make his decision, so he retired for five minutes to do this. Whilst he was gone, I went into a trance. In the trance—or you could even call it a vision—I saw myself sleeping on the bottom bunk of what looked like a prison cell. As soon as I saw it, I began to cry. This was my confirmation that my worst fear was going to happen to me. I knew the verdict before the judge entered the room. I looked at my friend, and she saw the tears roll down my face. The judge re-entered the room and delivered his verdict of four months custodial sentence. His explanation was that I was a clever girl and knew what I was doing. So he thought it would be the best form of punishment. He said regardless of the fact that I didn't have a criminal record (no previous convictions), he believed that this was best. The officers came and took me away. I was broken. My stomach was tying itself up in knots. Everything had happened so quickly. I couldn't register the fact that I was going to prison. I cried constantly. I couldn't do anything else. I couldn't even speak; all I could do was cry.

They took me down to the cells under the court because they had to call around and find a prison that had a space to house me. All that was going through my head was my parents. They were going to be heartbroken. "My mum and dad, oh God, my mum and dad," was all I kept crying and saying. I had seen the televi- sion show Bad Girls, but that was as far as my experience of prison went. I didn't know where I was going and what it was going to be like. The fear that came over me at that point was so strong. Questions were going through my mind. How would I be treated? What if they beat me up? What if they abused me? I just couldn't understand why this was happening. I knew I had done a crime a few years back, and now a few years later when I was getting my life back on track, they wanted to ruin everything. By they, I meant the law.

My lawyer came down to see me because he wanted me to sign some papers so that he could start the appeal process. All he kept saying was how sorry he was. He didn't understand how this had gone this way. He said everyone in the room, even the people who took me to court, were shocked at the outcome. All they wanted was for me to pay back the money, but instead he sent me to prison. I asked my lawyer to call my friend and my parents and let them know what had happened. He said he would. I didn't know how they were going to take it, but I wanted them to know as early as possible.

The officer came to the court cell to see me, and he said that they would be taking me to Foston Hall. Well, of course, I didn't know where that was. I didn't know what it was like, even though the officer assured me it was a hotel compared to loads of other locations. After about three hours, they came for me and took me to the van that would transport me to my new home for the next four months. If you saw the little cubicles that they lock you up in, you would know how a person couldn't even move. It was a one-hour journey, and I spent it reading all the graffiti that was etched into the cubicle walls and doors by people who had been in that same cubicle, on the same type of journey to their new home, for however long they had been sentenced to.

Finally, I reached the prison, and it actually looked quite nice on the outside. But I was still crying. At that time, I don't think there was anything that could have stopped me from crying. I was emotionally broken, going somewhere I knew nothing about. I was expected to adjust to this new environment that I didn't belong in. In my mind, I was just going over how I managed to reach there and battling with the fact that I was stuck there. Nothing I could do would change it, so I had to get used to it. I decided that I had to buck up my ideas and try and get on. There was nothing to be done now. All I could do was fit in and ride it until it was over.

They booked me in and I had to go through tests with the nurse before they settled me into a room. They took me down to the officers' room, and there they assigned me a room and gave me my room key. I was so upset and teary-eyed that they gave me a room near their office. They said they didn't want me to feel alone, so they would keep me near them. I didn't know what to do. I was escorted to my room. In there was an en suite shower and toilet, a television, wardrobe, and kettle. It was like a minimalistic hotel room; no wonder they said it was like a hotel. I had my own key to my room, and I didn't have to let anyone in who I didn't want in.

I sat at the desk in my room, staring at the wall. I didn't know what to do first. I had sheets provided so I could make my bed, but I just didn't feel like I could be bothered. I arrived in my room around dinnertime, but I didn't go to dinner because I didn't feel comfortable. I was scared of the other girls and how they would receive me. So I sat there, trying still not to cry. An officer came in and asked me if I was going for dinner, and I told her I was fine. She understood I was new and that I had never been to prison before, so she went and got food for me. After dinner, some of the girls realised that I was new and came in to see me. They were quite nosey, but, at the same time, friendly. They wanted to know all about me and what I had done. Most of all, they wanted me to be their friend. I know what you are thinking—it was prison and they would have made friends with anyone. But at that time, it meant a lot to me, because I was new to this kind of environment and didn't know where to start.

There was no way to fight my emotions. The only way I was able to express myself was through tears. The tears continued to flow; it was as if I was in overflow. I was yearning for a release, but I knew for sure that whilst I was in that situation, such release was not guaranteed. It took me a few days to properly get into the routine. On the first Sunday I was in, I went with the other girls to church. A lot of the girls only went to get off the wing, but it was that same yearning for peace that encouraged me to go. I remember sitting in the room, and we were singing all the songs from the olden days. I remembered them from when I used to go to school and they were playing tambourines and enjoying themselves. It was at the point of prayer time that I felt the tears flowing down my cheek. The impact of where I had found myself again hit me. All of a sudden, I felt a certain peace come over me, and the tears dried up. I felt comfortable. I felt as if God was saying,

"I have heard you, and I know what you are going through. But don't worry, I am with you."

I came out of that service feeling revived and unburdened. Even though I was still in the same situation as before I went in, there was a certain peace that surrounded me.

I started to interact with the other girls more and finally got into the way of living. After all, it hadn't been a week yet, and I had seven more weeks ahead of me. In English prisons when you are sentenced, you only do half the sentence, so even though I was given four months, I only had to serve two months which equated to eight weeks. I began to talk to God in my lonely times. I began to plan my future with Him and He with me. I think the fact that I was in a room by myself was a great help in enabling me to settle in quicker and more efficiently. It was while sitting at my desk within the first week that God spoke to me and gave me the title and chapters of this book that you are reading now. He gave me the topics and outlines of each chapter and where they would come, as well as insight into how I would write them. If you remember, it was about two years previously that God inspired me to write this book, but it wasn't the right time. In this situation, going through what I was going through, He was saying it was time to now plan the book, but not time to write. I spent two days getting the contents, titles, and so on in order, and then I put it away knowing that when it was time to write they would come in handy. At my desk, I wrote countless letters to friends and family expressing my feelings and saying how sorry I was for letting them down. I explained to them why I believed this had happened to me and how close I was getting to God because of it.

During the months leading up to this time, I had fallen so far away from God. I had no time for Him. Everything else seemed to be important, and He came last. This was the time to find my way back to His feet, to come back into alignment with His word and His plans for my life. I knew that where I was at the time was not where I was supposed to be. I even know now that where I am right now is not where I am supposed to be. Because of wrong choices, even whilst being saved, I have set myself back quite a bit. But I'm pressing forward to get to where I need to be in Christ.

I had to allow myself to be quiet for God to be able to speak to me. I needed silence to be able to hear His still, small voice. I was given the greatest opportunity whilst I was there to just be quiet, to just wait and hear Him respond to me. Sometimes I would just lie in my bed in the dark at night time and pray. And I would lie there, waiting just to hear one word. That one word would make the difference in my life for that day or the next day. Just to hear one word. And sure enough, God would always hon- our His word. He would speak, or I would receive some kind of revelation and insight into something. I learned so much over the time I was there. I was able to come to the place of total surrender, because there was nothing else I could do. It brought back a song to me called "I Surrender All." I truly did, and when I did, I began to see God work in the midst of my situation.

When I first went to prison, an officer had come to me and said that because I was not going to be there for long, they wouldn't move me to a wing. I would stay on that unit until my sentence was up. The unit I was on was called the Remand unit. Normally, you went there if you hadn't been sentenced or for the first few days before moved, as long as you are not a threat.

Anyway, one day when I was lying on my bed, just talking to God during lockdown, an officer opened my door told me to pack my things because I was moving. I looked at him and then at the bag, and I burst into tears. All of a sudden, the peace that took me so long to acquire had left me. It was like the day I came to prison all over again. They were moving me on to the main prison, to D Wing. As I said before, I had seen Bad Girls and knew what prison was like according to television programmes; based on that perspective, I didn't want to move. I felt a sharp pain cut across my stomach as I was crying out to God, asking him why. I was saying to God how He promised to look after me, and that He gave me peace as if everything was okay, so why would He allow them to move me? I went on and on and on in my pity party. I felt betrayed. I felt like God gave me a false sense of hope, and now I was being thrown into the lion's den, as Daniel had in the Bible.

They came to take me over to the new wing and I went quietly. I was not the kind of person to make a noise and protest about it. We went on a long walk over to the main prison, where I was placed into a room with three other women. Remember, I always went along quietly, but when they put me in with three smokers, they crossed the line. There was no way I was staying in there. I was scared to make noise the first day I went there, so I tried to live it out and prayed that the smoke wouldn't suffocate me in the night. But having to inhale the fumes and having no windows—in a room that was so small and stuffy already— nope, wasn't happening.

I spent the night in the room and couldn't wait until the next day to go to the office and ask them to get me out of there. I barely made it through the night. At the same time, I had a mattress on the bed that was so thin I might as well have been sleeping on the floor. That meant instant backache and tossing and turning the whole night, trying not to wake the others with my fidgeting.

The next day, I went straight to the office to complain and get them to move me. They blamed me for not speaking up, until they actually admitted that I was moved by mistake. When they sent for people to come over, they said they wanted smokers, and I was a nonsmoker. Obviously, I was happy at that and began to wonder if they would send me back to where I had come from. No such luck. They juggled around two other nonsmokers and put us in together. Not what I wanted, but it was better than being in a smoke-filled room.

I was moved in with an old lady and a vulgar, bully type of woman who frequented prison the way I breathed fresh air. I can't remember why the girl was in there, but the old lady was accused and sentenced for allegedly stealing pensioners twenty thousand pounds out of their house. Well, she declared her inno- cence, but I didn't know either way. I didn't want to get into the formalities with her. At the end of the day, she was there doing her time as everyone else in that place.

My parents and close friend came to visit me, which was my first visit since I was there. I was dreading going out there to see them; I didn't know what they were going to say or how they would view me. All I knew was that I couldn't cry. I had to be strong for their sake, even if I went back to my room and cried afterward. I just couldn't cry in front of them. The visit went quite well, and we all survived without crying. My mum brought me clothes and money for me to get by over the following five weeks. They just encouraged me and wanted me to know they were praying for me and then some. Well, as you can imagine, when I got back to my room, I cried for two hours. I never wanted them to come in the first place, because I never ever wanted them to see me in that position. I was ashamed of where I had reached. I had put them through so much over the years, and now I had changed my life around to doing good, but bad was still presenting itself. Things were still catching up with me from my past. When would it end? Would this be it? After this, would there be anything else to come and haunt me? God willing, no! After my visit, even thought it made me teary eyed, I felt supported. And even though I knew I had let my parents down, they were there for me through thick and through thin.

Over time, I became quite close to the old lady who I was sharing the room with. We signed up to coffee mornings and an arts and craft women's group that was hosted by the chaplaincy. I encouraged her to come to church, which she wasn't used to, but I decided that whilst I was there I knew God wanted me to help somebody.

Sunday came around so quickly, and I had been in prison for eleven days. I woke up bright and early and decided I was going to church—and my new friend was coming with me.

While walking into the chapel, and I heard them singing,

"I'm coming back to the heart of worship."

This song touched my heart, because whilst I had been in prison, I had been speak- ing to God and telling Him those same words. I was confessing to Him and asking Him to help me to come back in line with His word and back to the heart of worship. The speaker was talking about His sheep knowing His voice, and another they will not follow. It was so relevant to my current situation and, again, what God and I had been conversing about. That morning, I again left church with peace that passed all understanding. Yet again, I was still in the same situation, but God heard me and was working on my behalf. I had felt alone and neglected, but God had never left me. He was still always there. He was doing His thing in the background. It was just that my faith wasn't big enough to see Him operating on my behalf.

I was believing God for a miracle, but at the same time, I came to the realisation that, if I had to continue with this sentence, God would give me the grace and strength to see it through. Even if He didn't take me out of it, He was still God and He was still faithful.

I got through the weekend and was surprised to receive a letter from my solicitor on Monday morning. It was confirming my appeal court date and the whole procedure. I hadn't even remembered that I had signed the papers for appeal the day I was sentenced. The letter was saying that I was due in the Crown Court on that Thursday for my hearing. Thursday! It was so soon. But even thought it was soon, time had gone so slowly. It's not like now, when one week goes so fast that you get the days mixed up. As I previously explained, one day was like one week. I got excited and called my mum to tell her what was happening. I thanked God for this sign, and I knew He was going to do something spectacular in my life. The general belief amongst the officers and inmates was that I would get released, because I had no previous convictions. But I was not taking it as likely to happen. Yes, that might have been the case, but if it was down to that information alone, I wouldn't have been in there in the first place.

Over the following days, I just prayed that God would give me strength and that His will would be done in my life. Every time I proclaimed what I believed, there would always be a small voice telling me I was stupid and that I was coming straight back to prison from court. But I couldn't let those negative voices bring me down. All I needed was faith as small as a mustard seed, and I had it. It wasn't big, but it was enough.

9
This is It

On the sixteenth of April in 2008, everyone said "bye" to me and wished me luck with my court date the next day. People I had not even spoken to before were wishing me well for my future, as they had been observing me from afar and knew I was a nice person. The old lady I was sharing a cell with was encour- aging me to have faith and saying that everything would be okay. She said that I will be fine and free the next day. Going through my mind was happiness, because I believed that, yes, I would be free the next day. But there was that little voice in the back of my head saying that I would be returning back to prison and that maybe this next judge would send me back for more time. But I persevered. The vulgar woman had been moved out of the room and replaced by a very upset and bewildered Chinese girl. She didn't really understand what was going on, but she knew I was in court, but I think she was so over whelmed with what was going on in her own life that she wished she was going home. I sat and spoke to her and assured her she would be okay, that she will be home soon with her family. From the day she came into our room, she cried. She was overwhelmed with emotion. She did not want to be there, but it couldn't be helped; she was there for a reason. It was just a point of encouraging her to stay strong because, at the end of the day, when all is said and done, she would be home with her family soon.

I went to bed that night and could not sleep. I was experiencing mixed emotions. I was happy and scared at the same time. I was journeying into the unknown. My life was not in my hands, but it was in God's hands. Every thought, every emotion did not matter, because God was in control. I entrusted Him with my life. I let go and allowed Him to take control. As much as I never knew what the outcome would be, I believed it was going to be positive, because I knew the God in whom I believed. My faith was the size of a mountain. I knew deep down I was going to be okay.

It was about five thirty a.m., and the wardens came around to wake me up so I could get ready. I was awake already, just lying there thinking into space. I could not tell what time it was; I woke up at approximately four a.m. I was lost in a trance; I was meditating on life and partly on my pending court case.

I got out of bed, had a wash, and got dressed slowly. As I was preparing myself, I was looking at the two ladies I was leaving behind. I felt sorry for them because I was leaving them there. I wished I could have taken them with me, but I couldn't. All I could do was pray that God would keep them safe in His care and that one day they would come to know Him personally. Finally, I was ready to go and the wardens came back around to collect me. I said my good-byes to the ladies and then left the room. There was a girl opposite me who also was in Derby court, so we were travelling together. She was a drug addict from Derby who, as far as I could remember, I had never seen before. But she frequented around the "ends" that I used to hang around, and she knew some of the same people that I knew. I never spoke to her whilst we were together, but I say it was destiny and bound that we should speak. You may ask why, but I am about to tell you.

We travelled in these little cubicles from Foston Hall Prison to Derby Crown Court, the journey lasting about forty-five minutes. I spent my time reading all the scrawl that people before me had left in there. People from all walks of life all over the United Kingdom voiced their opinions and left their tag where others who came later could see they had been there, a bit like graffiti.

When we reached Derby, I was emotional, as you can imagine. Then something strange happened. The officer at the court asked me if I wanted to go in and share a cell with the girl I had travelled with from Foston Hall. I was so shocked at her question. I did not know what to say. Asking a prisoner where she would like to go is not normally an option. So in response, and bearing in mind I was in shock, I said I did not mind. So she put us together.

I sat next to this woman, and we started to dialogue with each other. She told me a bit about herself, and I told her about me and my background. She had suffered from pneumonia a short time previously and nearly died. She had a heavy drug problem and had lost her daughter to a freak accident in Derby five years previously. I felt so burdened as she was telling me her story; my heart was moved with compassion. I did not know what to say or do. When we first started talking, I told her about my faith in God and what He had done for me, so it prompted her to tell me about her experiences with God. I could tell by her heartrending story that it was cutting her to pieces. Her daughter was her everything, and then when she was killed, it was as if her world ended. She became an alcoholic, started knocking around with other drug addicts, and became dependant on drugs herself. She started thieving, which is how she had been in and out of prison for the past couple of years. And if she got bail that day, she had another theft charge to answer to. So they would send her back to prison anyway.

Here in front of me was a broken woman, attacked by tragedy, and she did not look like she was going to get better. When we finished talking, we ended up quite close. A short conversation, and we knew so much about each other. And then she dropped the big one. She asked that we pray together. She said she understood God was there, and she knew He was calling her into the faith. She strongly believed that it was because of God that we had met, and maybe I was there for her. At that time, in my head I was asking God if He would really have put me through this for a soul … and the answer, which was whispered to me, was yes. From that I knew I was going home. My doubts were settled. I did not have to go through all this; the crime took place so long ago and I had moved on, even repented, and took myself out of the situation. But God allowed it to happen for a reason.

I suggested that we both pray and she should begin. She began to pray, and whilst she was doing so, I was asking God to direct my words. I did not want to go off on a tangent and say big words or talk about what she did not know. I wanted her to understand what I was sending up to Heaven on her behalf. I started by presenting each of us to God and our situations. Then I got to a specific part. I said, "Lord, do not allow the judge to see us and our past; do not let him judge us on what we have done and where we have been, but allow him to see where we could be and where we are going." That section of my prayer moved me. As I was speaking those words that I will never forget, I felt the presence of God in such a profound way. I felt the vibration of the Holy Spirit. He was there with us, to the point where I heard the lady say, "Wow, you don't understand what I just felt when you were talking about them not judging me from where I have been or what I had done." At that point, she claimed her faith in God had been restored and made a promise that if she got bail, she would meet me at my church Sunday morning. The presence of God filled the room, and we felt His comfort. It was just me and her, and we knew something was happening in the atmosphere.

The warden came in as my barrister and lawyer wanted to see me. I went out to see them in a special room. I was introduced to my barrister, and she told me about my case and the proceedings of the day. She laid two options on the table. She wanted me to decide what I wanted to do. As I had only three weeks left on my sentence, she said I could just go back to prison and finish it, knowing that in three weeks I would be free forever or I could go into court and go before the judge. If I went before the judge, he could suspend my sentence and could give me community service, or he could see it fit to extend my sentence. My barrister did not think it was worth it to take those kinds of chances and advised me to go back to prison and ride out the final three weeks. She asked me for my decision. Time seemed to all of a sudden go really slow; it almost stopped. Instantly, a thought was brought back to my memory. Whilst I was locked up, I got a book from the chapel called My Daily Bread. It was a daily devotional book that I found really helpful whilst I was there. One day, I was reading about a class of students and a teacher. They had come to the end of the semester, and the teacher said to them that she would give them all an A without them doing their end of semester exam because they had worked so hard all year, or they could take the exam. The students had a decision to make, but had to battle with the possibility that they could get less than an A. So taking the A without putting the hard work in was good. Ninety-five percent of the class decided to take the free grade and did not do the exam. The five percent who took the exam got an automatic A+. They had faith that they would try their best to get what they could. If they got less than an A, at least they tried. But they were determined to try and not take the easy way out. And they were duly awarded for trying. In exchange for not being comfortable, they got a better grade than if they had settled for the easier option.

So now I was faced with this option: take the easy route and go back to where I had come from or go forward, stepping into the unknown. I had to make a decision based on what I didn't know, as opposed to what I knew was for sure. So I did. I told them that, no matter what, I was going into that court room. I put my complete trust in God that His will would be done in my life that day, and I believed He would come through for me. So, to their shock and non-agreement, they sent me back to my cell until it was my turn to go up to court.

I got back to my cell and talked to my newfound friend until we had to go our separate ways. She gave me her address, and we made promises to each other to keep in contact even if we didn't get bail, because we believed that this would be a great friendship that God had brought us to. Not long after I returned to the cell, they came back for me to go up into court. I said my good-byes to my friend and boldly went up to be taken into the court. The officer who took me up was quite friendly, asking me about my case and what I had done. When I told her, she was in total shock that the previous judge had ordered me to prison. I explained to her the attitude of the judge and that everyone I came across was shocked at the outcome. But I was believing for freedom this day. I went into the courtroom and stood before the judge. He seemed nice and friendly and spoke nice things about me, even though he did not know me other than from the file he had read on me. My eyes filled up with tears on every word that he spoke. I was fighting to hold back the tears, but I just became so overwhelmed and emotional. This man, who I had never met in my life, spoke some things about me that morning that, as I write this now, still have me in shock. He said that I was someone who had a bright future in front of me. I had many opportunities, which it looked like I would utilise, and could be someone great. He encouraged me to go home to a family who loved me and pursue my future in whatever field it was that I was exploring. He wished me all the best for the future and knew I was sorry for what I had done so long ago. He did not want to take any more time away from me. He gave me a suspended sentence for twelve months and, instead of giving me community service, he told me I had to see a proba- tion officer for twelve months, just to make sure I am coping.

I was ecstatic! No one could wipe the smile off my face. I was so happy, the tears started to roll down my face. There was no stopping me, and I thanked God so much. I had taken that chance based upon what I had read whilst exploring God's word, and my God came through for me. He was faithful and true, and I can never ever thank Him enough for all He did—and is still doing in my life today.

I left the courtroom and they took me to get my things and fill out some paperwork. Then that was it. They ushered me out of the building. I remember walking out of the front of the building and seeing Derby city centre. I was so happy that I ran with the bag. I did not know what to do first, bearing in mind I had a big HMP bag that was see-through. I decided I did not want anyone to see me with it, so I jumped in a taxi and went straight home. I was so happy in the taxi, and I knew my parents would be excited to see me. We drove down all these roads and passed people I knew, and I was just happy to see them and be in the area because I was free. It had only been two weeks, but it felt like years. Trust me, the time had gone so slowly for me whilst I was locked up, but now I was free.

We arrived outside my house, I paid the taxi driver, and approached my house. I stepped over to the door and knocked on it. My mum answered; there was happiness that filled the house. Joy overflowed. Smiles and praises went up to God. My parents were so happy to see me come home. They said they had been praying hard and knew I would come through the door. Instantly, I plugged my phones in and charged them up, because I wanted to text my pastor and tell her I was home, as well as contacting some friends who were worried about me. They were all so happy to hear from me. They couldn't believe I was home. Yes, I was living proof that God was still on the throne.
Finally, I was able to get my life back on track. This was the first day of the rest of my life. Everything that had gone on and happened before this day was buried. I left it in the past. All the bad decisions, all the heartbreak, unforgiveness, hurt, and pain; I left it there because I knew that I was going to live every day as if it was my last. My dream had become large. I was visualising things and speaking things into my life that seemed impossible. I assured myself that I was going to make all my dreams come through by the grace of God, because I knew and believed

that I could do all things through Christ who gave me strength. And I still believe that today.

I got back into church life and found that my praises were more resounding. I had things to thank God for before, but now He had turned my whole life around. He brought me out of the miry clay and put me on a rock to stay. I could never thank Him enough. Till the day I die, I know that I could never praise Him enough for all He had done for me and all He is going to do for me in my future.

I felt so much closer to God when I came back. I attribute this closeness to the fact that, for the two weeks I was away, I made my meditation about Him, my thoughts and conversation all were in line with Him, and what I was believing Him for. I realised that I had no one but Him. Everything I had ever tried in life had failed me, but one thing stood sure continually—God and His unfailing love for me. You may ask what makes me so special that God would love me. Well, let me tell you something: He does not just love me; He loves you too. God has enough love for every single person in this world, if we just believe and trust in Him. He does not want to hurt us, but make us happy and give us life everlasting. Christianity isn't boring, as some people believe. You can still have fun, live your life, and be in a two-way relationship with the Maker.

Christianity is not about a religion, because I am no way religious. I was brought up in church all my life and couldn't serve God because I thought He was boring and that I could not live my life. It wasn't until I came back to a place of receiving Him again that He showed me a different side to Him. I saw the fun side of God. I wasn't dry and stiff; I was happy, having fun and still living right. Trust me, whatever pre-conceptions you have about going to church, I bet I could prove you wrong. But, hey, I'm not here to preach you into the Kingdom. I am telling you of my experience.

So where was I? Oh, yeah!

I always wanted to continue to set up my own business in event management, and God gave me the inspiration to look into what I would have to do to accomplish it. I looked into courses that I could do to give me qualifications and experience and then enrolled. In the midst of studying, I also got myself back into university to finish my degree in Business and Computing. It seemed like a lot of work, but I knew I was able to do it because I felt as if I had an infusion of strength. I realised life was short and decided that I was going to do all I could do to fulfill it. There was never any point in being cautious; as long as I was not breaking the law or the law of God, it was fine. Education has always and will always be the key. The Bible says,

"My people are destroyed by lack of knowledge."

With knowledge we are able to unlock all doors. We can go past all the boundaries and reach the highest mountain. This is something that I was beginning to understand and run after. I mentioned that while I was in prison, God told me to write down some topics and notes in regards to this book. He wanted me to write about my life story, so I got the papers out one evening and started to write. I experimented with a dictating machine so that I could record and then type, but I just couldn't get into it. So I just wrote down all the chapters, then sectioned them out, and started to type. It was so easy! I knew what I was writing about they were my memories and it was just flowing.

I then spent a few months setting up my Web site and sorting out business paperwork that was detrimental. And in the midst of it all. God had another plan to compliment me. I received a text message from my church secretary, asking me if I was working at that point in time. Well, if you remember, I had left my job in January because I couldn't take it anymore. So I replied and told her, no, I wasn't working, just trying to sort out setting up my business. She asked me to help her in the office at church with some tasks, because we had a conference coming up and she would have been really busy. I happily agreed. I didn't mind helping out in God's house. After all, I like helping people and admin work was a joy for me to do. A few days turned into a few weeks, which turned into a few months, and then turned into permanent—and I am not sorry. The day I started working for my church voluntarily was the greatest day of my life. I have never felt so fulfilled doing something. It was as if I was waiting all my life for this to happen. As strange as it sounds, I felt comfortable working as many hours as I had to, in order to get work done.

Even though it was voluntary, it satisfied me and I never struggled. I was able to meet my bills every month by the help of God and my parents. I had car that was expensive to maintain, and then some, but I was never in need. God supplied all my need. They say, "The blessings of the Lord maketh one rich and addeth no sorrow," and let me tell you, it is a true word. He supplied all my needs. The more time I spent at church doing God's work, the more knowledge and wisdom I attained. It is a known fact that if you hang with fools, you turn a fool.
You always have to be careful who you associate with, as their attitudes, actions, and character will rub off on you. So if you want to be wise, you hang with wise people. If you want to know how to be a

millionaire, you need to hang with other millionaires. I am still working on the millionaire one, but it's coming. This is because I went to a meeting led by televangelist Juanita Bynum in June 2008, and she spoke to me, and said that I was going to be a millionaire, but it wouldn't come from nothing. I would have to work hard for it and pray a lot. Now, one thing I do not like is prayer. You may be freaked out right now, wondering what I am coming off with, but I am being honest. Sometimes I find it so hard to break through in prayer. My heart's desire even now is to be able to enter into prayer and have things happen, but I was at the stage where I would be clock-watching. I started praying, asking God to help me to love prayer. I still pray that prayer now, and gradually I am getting better day by day. Prayer is a necessity and I need to be able to love it. I don't want it to seem like a chore to pray; it is so important to me. Sometimes.

I believe that's why I have so many trials because trials and tribulations teach you to pray. It's a part of life. Even people who are not Christians will admit that when there are troubles in their lives, they are driven to say a prayer. The more trials I have, the more I pray. So in a way, the trials have helped my prayer life. But I need to be able to stand in prayer when I haven't got troubles … and I know it's coming.

I was reminded of when I went to the singles camp in 2007, during which a word was spoken into my life by one of the brothers. A part of what he said was that "I would go places and rub shoulders with people I would never imagine." The conference was the beginning of that for me. I went places and was exposed to certain atmospheres that I would not normally be in. God said to me that this was not all He had planned for me. It was just a taste. He was just reminding me of the prophecy that was given and letting me know to still believe, because He had not forgotten and was working it all out for me. If you were to ask me five years ago where I would be now, I don't know what I would have said. My relationship with my husband was not that bad at the time, and I probably thought I would still be with him, happily married and kids. But God worked it out completely differently.

Every day that I live and breathe, I know God is working out purpose in my life. My destiny is already fulfilled in God. It was written and complete before the foundations of the Earth. I just need to catch up with it now. God is awesome is all I can say. Every day that I wake up is a miracle in itself.

During our conference, it was the most awesome experience. We were challenged to come up higher, because our hour had come. Friends, my hour truly did come. I had been looking for a job from when I had left my job in January, and nothing was happening. I had all the experience, but I couldn't get a job. I would go for interviews and then something would happen to the interviewer so they couldn't get back to me or something else bizarre. It came to the point where I had to ask God if He was trying to tell me something, because I was the kind of person who, when I went for a job, I always got it. I never ever got turned down, so what had changed? My mum was getting frustrated and kept on asking if I wasn't going to get a job. I honestly was trying, but then getting distressed as well, because I couldn't get a breakthrough. Whilst I was helping at church, I put my business plans on hold so I could fully concentrate, and I even stopped writing this book.

On the last night of our conference, Bishop Walter Smith spoke a word. He said that someone had been looking for a job for about six months and that it looked as if this person couldn't get a breakthrough. As soon as I heard that, I wanted to cry. He then said that God said to stop looking and do His work. I was thinking to myself, What does that mean? Stop looking and do God's work? I had to ask God what He was saying, as this made no sense to me. I was questioning, wanting to know how I would pay my bills and if I had heard correctly. I just did not understand what I was going to do with no job. It was later on in the week, when God spoke into my spirit and I realised that He had put me in the position of administration for a reason. Even today, I am still unfolding that reason. But it is doing His work, His will. This is what God wants for me at this point in my life.

As time went on after the conference, my mum was still asking when is the job coming and was even looking for me. I was finding it hard to tell her what God said. I didn't feel confident to say it. When people in general used to ask me if I was working, I would say I am just working for church at the moment, voluntarily. A lot of them used to look at me as if to say, "What do you mean, voluntarily?" They would never say it, but I knew what they were thinking. Sometimes I felt so down that I wasn't working at a paying job that I would feel like looking for a job, just to see if I could get anything. But something would always stop me and remind me that, even if I did, I wouldn't get it because it was not in God's plan. How crazy is that? I really wanted to work and God was saying "no." I was really battling with the fact that I was not working, and one night I had a dream that my senior pastor was in the admin office, and he was talking to me and the church secretary about when, in the Bible, Jesus said that we should occupy until He comes. Then the pastor turned to me and said, "Jesus said you must occupy until He comes." All of a sudden, the secretary turned to me and raised her voice at me, almost shouting at me, saying "Did you not hear what God said? He said you must stop looking for work and do His work." I mean, how much clearer would you really need it? God had to reaffirm

His word to me because I had doubts. I was letting what people say about my situation get to me. If I had not had this dream, I don't know what I would have done when what was going to happen did happen later on in the week.

I went to the home of someone from church and, during our conversation, she switched and asked me what I was doing. Well, of course, considering that she was a church member, I thought she would understand. So I told her that I was volunteering for church, and the first thing she said to me was, "What's the point if you're not getting paid?" I was shocked at what she said, because I just did not expect it from her, of all people. How would I get across to her the fact that it was worth it because I was doing it for God, not man? Her response just didn't warrant me to have a conversation at all with her. I just wanted to get up and leave her house, but I couldn't because I didn't want to be rude. I felt like the inner battle was beginning again, but I had to remember the dream I was given. Every time the thought came to me to buy a paper and look for a job, I remembered that God said to "do His work." Later on in the week, again I had another confrontation, but this time from my sister. We were having a perfectly normal conversation, and then all of a sudden out of nowhere, it was like someone had charged her up. She just started flying off the handle at me, as if I had done something to her. She cursed me off about the fact that I was driving a car and paying bills with government money and, therefore, she was paying for me to live because she has to pay her taxes. She was saying how nothing was wrong with me, so why couldn't I work and how God would not be happy, because He says I should work and pay tithes to Him. The flesh of me wanted to rise up and give her a piece of my mind and curse her off, but I just sat there and lis- tened. Then when it was my turn to speak, I think

I said one word and the phone cut off. I realised God did not want me to respond at that point, but I texted her anyway, telling her how I would never ring back her phone. I told her that if she wanted an answer to her questions, she must ask God and He would give it to her. I knew she wouldn't, because she isn't in a relationship with God. I was a bit naughty, because I said in the text message that if she was at the place with God or in a relationship with God, it wouldn't be so bad. But she wasn't, so she wouldn't understand God or even know when He is speaking. God forgive me, but she hurt my feelings.

One thing I learned through the whole experience was that if God said He would do it, He will. And it won't just happen because He said so. I have to say it. I have to believe it, receive it, and say it back. God spoke a word into my spirit one day during all this mess that was going on around me, and He said, "Multiple streams of income." I kept on hearing it over a few days. I had a friend that I held dear to me, and we were talking and decided to go into business together. She is a clothes designer and I am business- minded. We wanted to open a bridal wear shop. We didn't know how and where, but we had the feeling. The rest was up to God to lead us, as we were going to seek Him in prayer. "Multiple streams of income, multiple streams of income." That's all I heard and was not shocked when my friend confirmed to me that the Lord had been speaking the same words in to her spirit also.

I remember during the first business meeting we had, she told me about a dream she had had, which was unrelated to the business, but a name that was mentioned in the dream was the name that was on my mind to call the business. It was bizarre! I knew everything was going to work together. We had faith as small as a mustard seed, and we just couldn't wait to see this thing grow. We had our first meeting a week

prior to me writing this, and we are currently setting up what we need to and go through all the important paperwork that needs to be done. By the time this book hits the shelves, we hope to be up and running.
The question is: where am I now and where do I go from here? Well, it is all in my saviour's hands. I trust Him with my life.

I have my event management business, which I am pushing through; the new venture for an online business, which is going through; I am studying part-time; I am working part-time for my church, which I will never give up; and I have this book, which you are partaking in now as I write. There is a whole lot more to come; it has been spoken into my life. I am making sure to hang on every word, because they came from the throne room of God. I ensure to speak what He promised me back to Him as often as possible. I know He hasn't forgotten, but sometimes you just need to be in agreement with the Holy Spirit.

Let me tell you that I read a book on prayer by Bishop Clarence McClendon, and I will never be the same. Struggling to pray is getting less and less. It was the discovery of learning how to pray that enabled me to grasp the concept and open the door to an easier prayer life.
I want a family one day, and I want all the nice things— house, plush car, debt-free lifestyle—but most of all, I want to be pleasing to God. I want to walk in His light and, through that light, help people who are in situations like I have been through to realise that there is a way out. Just because you made a wrong turn or you were beaten or you are divorced, it does not mean that you cannot have the life you always wanted. I am a living testimony that, against the odds, you can make a comeback. When you think you are out for the count, you can get back up again. You can live to see another day. I love my parents. And because they had me late

in life, I always said to God that I wanted to be successful in life and make them proud before they are not around anymore. I want my kids to at least know their grandparents, I want them to be around for a lot longer, and I pray every day that God will keep them in His ever loving care. But I want to also be assured that I made them proud. After all the worry and all the pain, I want to be assured that I surpassed their expectations, knowing all the while that I could not have done any of this if it had not been for Jesus, if He didn't die for me so I could have life, and if I had not entered into the best relationship of my life.

The opportunities for me in life are endless. I want to help others who have given up on life. If I hadn't go through what I did, I could not assure you that it will be okay. If I did not have experience, then I would not be justified to speak to you, but here I am. I have poured out my soul. I became transparent so it can help people all over the world who feel like they cannot go another day. You have just travelled a twenty-five-year journey with me. If I can make it, you can. No limits … No boundaries …

My Friend

by Leanne Burke

My Friend, my life, my love,
In peace, in stillness, in troubles wild, I know that You are there;
To show me how to wait, slow down, To take away my fears.

When I feel alone, almost in deep despair, These are the times I feel, as if there's no one there.
The internal pain is amplified, by the sound of each new tear, A sound that I remember, a scar that feels so tender.

Every day I always pray that I'll be guided and not lose my way, My footsteps ordered night and day,
My hope that I will not stray,
But always help me remember the day, You sat me down and bid me stay.

The words You spoke so clear to me, that I may too forever be free,
You said You knew the plans for me, to make me strong and win, And even when I felt so far, as if all hope had gone,
I always came back to the one, where I get my strength from.

So as I go from day to day, I always know one thing, You lead me through the pain and strain, Straight to my destiny.

So when the tears and worry come, to take away my Joy, I lift my eyes up to the hills, that's where my safety lies,
In You is where I put my faith, in You I know I am complete.

I know in You my friend, my love, You hold my destiny, And through this love and friendship dear,
You bring me to the place, where I believe in me; And You, enable me to win!

10
All things are possible to those that believe...

Finally want to encourage you to move forward confidently in the same direction of your dreams. No matter what is going on around you I want to inspire you to live the life you have imagined. Your dreams may seem so far out of reach that you really do not believe that they can come true, but be assured that if I can be sitting here writing this and living my dreams today after all I have been through; you definitely can. I didn't tell you my story for sympathy, but to be able to use my mess and turn it into a message of hope. When things go wrong as they sometimes will, and when you feel like you are struggling uphill, your funds may be low and your debts very high, and you would do anything to smile, but all you can do is sigh. When you feel like the cares of this world are pressing you down, you can rest if you need to, but never ever quit. Life has its ups and its downs, and over time we always learn whilst many failures come about, but in reflection we realise that we may have won if we stuck it out. Do not give up even when things seem to be going slow, just continue to press forward and know that you could succeed with that next blow. Look at success being failure turned inside out, and understand that you will never know how close you really are. You may be so near even though it feels so very far, so I implore you to stick to the fight when you fell hardest hit, because it is in the times when things seem worst that you must not quit.

I always wanted to be one of those people that yes motivated, inspired and encouraged others, but I also wanted to be touchable. It is ok giving people advice and telling them this is how you did it, but it's not as straightforward for everyone. What if they need a physical touch or conversation? Sometimes they don't know who to turn to but your story connected to them and they feel you may be able to guide them. Being real is a major thing for me, because that is what the world needs. They don't want people telling them it is ok when they don't understand what they are going through and they don't want people acting like they have never had a problem in the world becuse everyone has problems. all i know is that If I did it and I am still doing it, then anyone can. All things are possible.

●

It is now 2012 and since writing this book in 2009, I have done television and radio interviews regarding my journey. I was also able to close the door on my past hurts and allow God to heal me from them. This in turn helped me to make the decision to be baptized—an outward show of the inward work. It took me three years to get there but I don't regret it. Life couldn't be better, and I owe it all to a man named Jesus.

I have also found my purpose in life and I am on the journey to becoming all God intended me to be. The Leanne Burke Show has been born, I am a Radio Presenter on a worldwide platform, I am in my last year of a Broadcast Media Degree, there are more books on the horizon and I am a motivational speaker. My purpose was born out of alot of pain, the pain of abuse and wrong choices that I made in my life. I came through all of that, to appear at this point in my life, stronger and ready to help others do the same.

One thing I know for sure is that I could never have made it this far without my faith in God.

I thank each and every one of you for coming on my life journey with me through this book, and especially if you lived my journey with me in reality.

I just want to remind you that change cannot occur unless you ignite it; unless you say so, it won't happen. Remember that life and death are in the power of the tongue. So speak life into all your situations and circumstances this day by faith. I have been through it. It was the fight of my life, but now, after the storm, I can say I understand why. I am a better person for all my trials. I am a stronger person for all my pain. Officially, I know the purpose in all of my pain.

Love you loads, Lee xxx

Lightning Source UK Ltd.
Milton Keynes UK
UKOW051725050912

198514UK00001B/49/P

KI PPERS

Gymnastics

Tim Wood

Kingfisher Books

Kingfisher Books, Grisewood and Dempsey Ltd,
Elsley House, 24–30 Great Titchfield Street,
London W1P 7AD.

First published in 1989 by Kingfisher Books

BRITISH LIBRARY CATALOGUING IN PUBLICATION DATA
Wood, Tim
Gymnastics
1. Gymnastics. For children
I. Title
796.4′1
ISBN 0-86272-381-7

Designed by Chris Hart
Edited by Jenny Wood
Illustrated by Lynne Willey/*John Martin & Artists Ltd*;
Amanda Appleby/*Maggie Mundy;*
Drawing Attention; Peter Stephenson/
Jillian Burgess

Phototypeset by Southern Positives and
Negatives (SPAN), Lingfield, Surrey
Printed in Spain

Contents

If you find an unusual or difficult word in this book, check for an explanation in the glossary on pages 30 and 31.

The Competition

The crowd falls silent as Clare takes up the starting pose for her floor routine. The music begins, and Clare springs lightly across the mat doing a series of flips which end in a perfect double backward somersault. There is a roar of applause. On the other side of the hall, John is finishing his exercise on the horizontal bar. All eyes turn to the scoreboard. Will Clare and John win?

.0.50
10.00
Skilful gymnasts make difficult exercises look easy. As you read this book you will find out how gymnasts build up the skills, confidence and courage they need in order to perform well.

How it all Began

Many centuries ago, the Ancient Greeks built the first special buildings for physical exercise. These were called ‘gymnasia’. The founder of modern gymnastics was Friedrich Jahn, a German school teacher, who opened the first open-air gymnasium in 1811. By 1896 gymnastics was a well-established sport and was included in the first modern Olympic Games in Athens, the capital city of Greece.

Travelling acrobats entertained people in China over 2000 years ago.

The 'Bull Dancers' of Ancient Crete performed dangerous acrobatic tricks.

During the Middle Ages, acrobats and tumblers like these performed at fairs and festivals.

Modern Gymnastics

The three main branches of modern gymnastics are artistic gymnastics, rhythmic gymnastics and sports acrobatics. Artistic gymnasts perform on pieces of apparatus. At a competition, the apparatus is set out on a large platform called a podium.

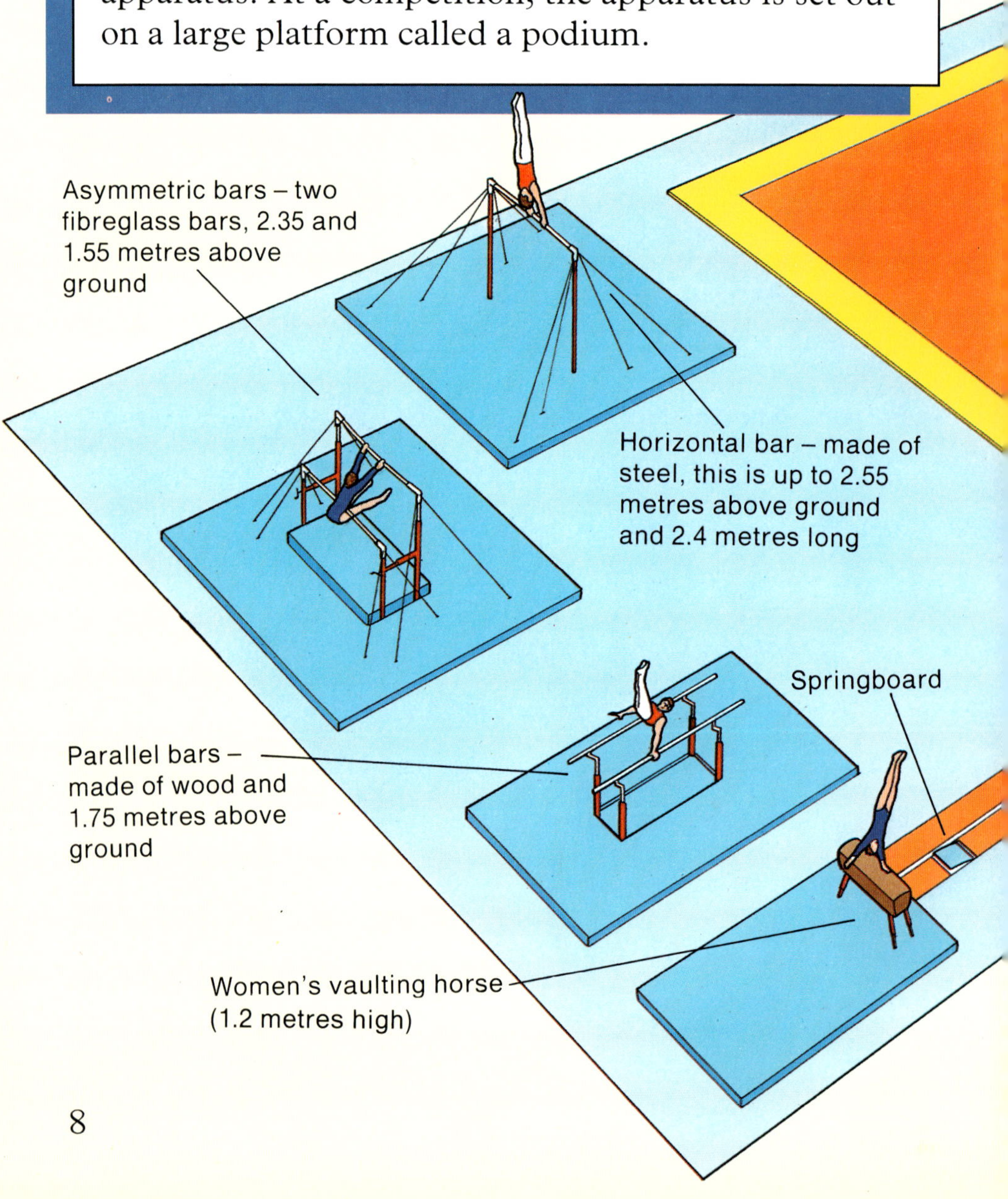

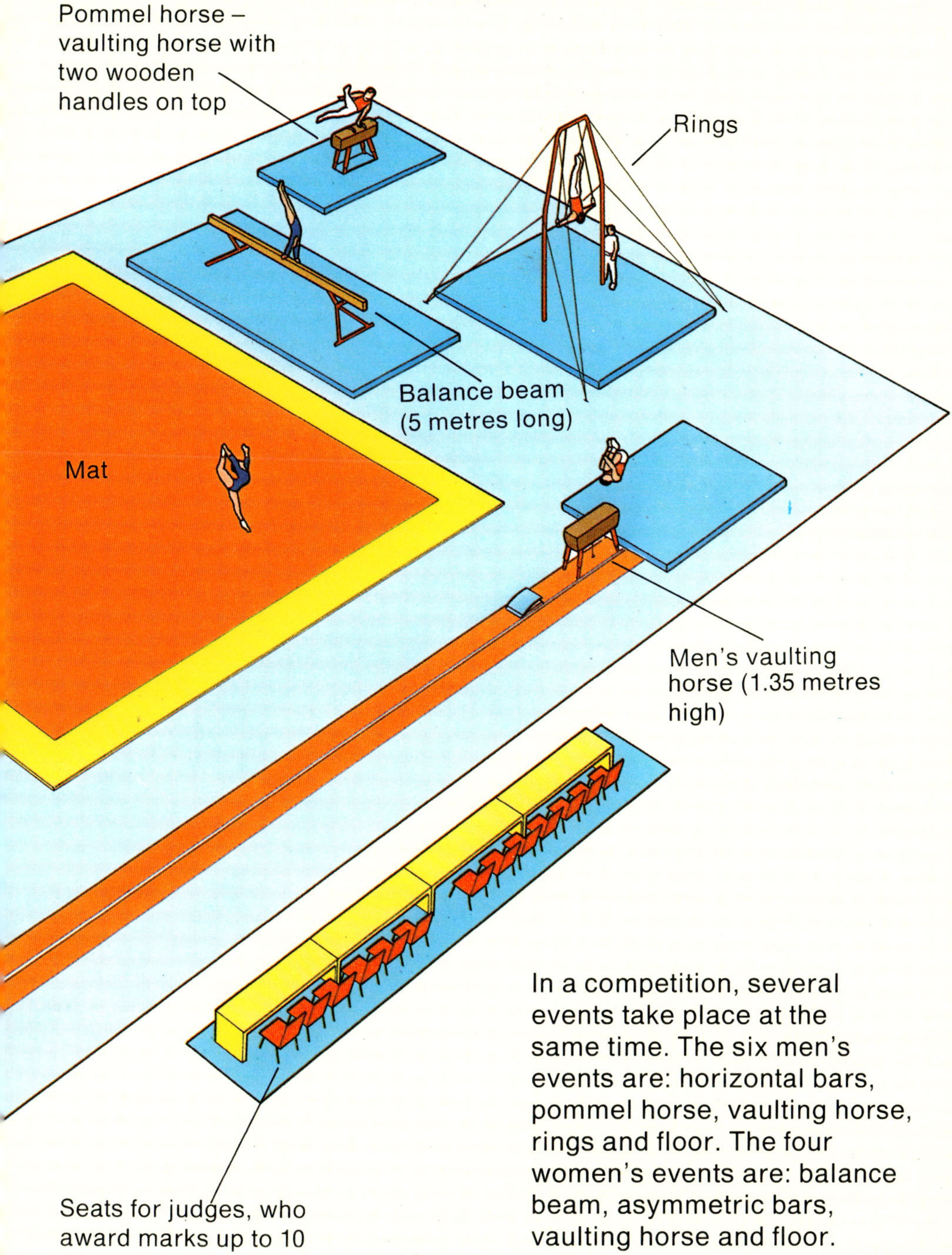

In a competition, several events take place at the same time. The six men's events are: horizontal bars, pommel horse, vaulting horse, rings and floor. The four women's events are: balance beam, asymmetric bars, vaulting horse and floor.

Beam and Bars

Women artistic gymnasts use four pieces of floor apparatus, including the asymmetric bars, which are bars set at different heights, and a wooden balance beam about 1 metre high. The gymnast jumps up to perform on the flat top of the beam. Exercises include walking and running steps in both directions, and balances, jumps and leaps.

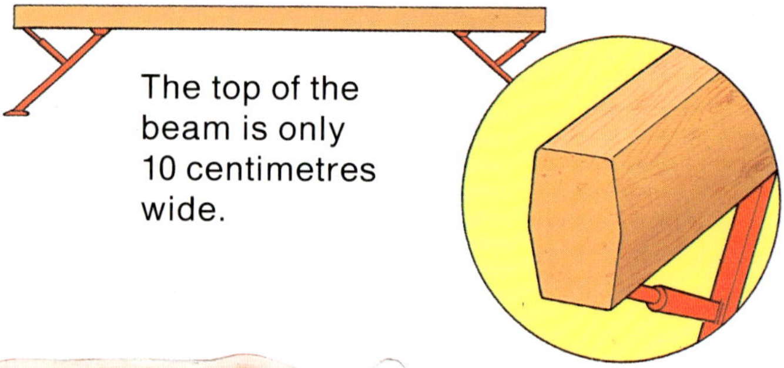

The top of the beam is only 10 centimetres wide.

A gymnast on the beam

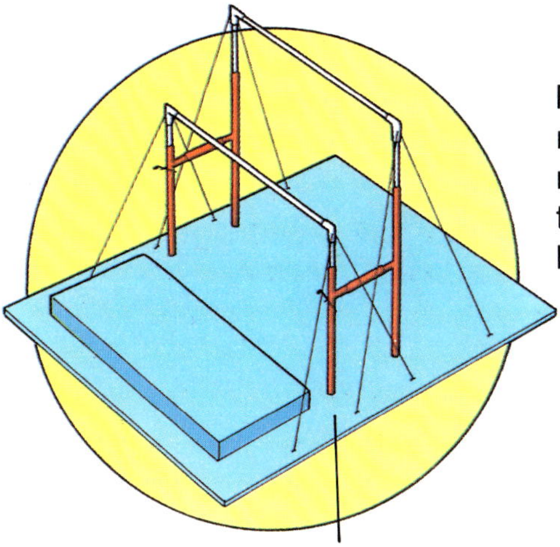

Asymmetric bars

Part of the routine must be on the high bar.

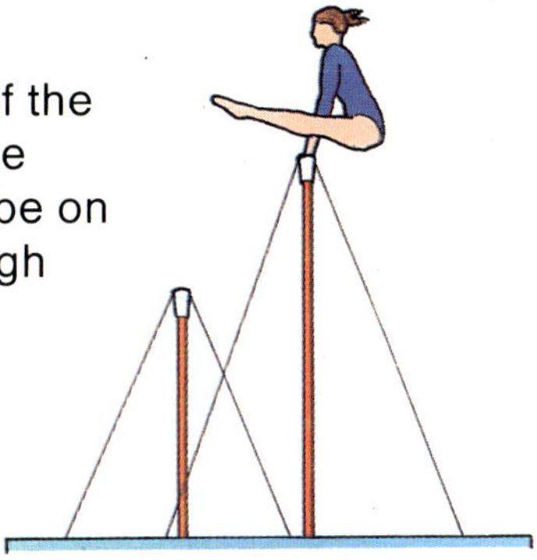

Gymnasts swing from bar to bar.

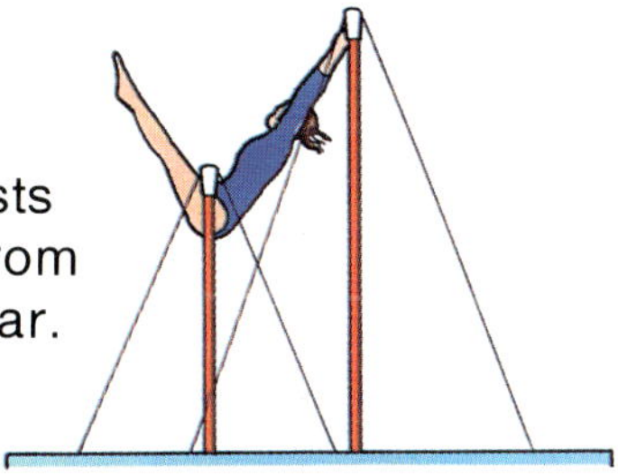

Part of the routine must be on the low bar.

Gymnasts must be strong and have excellent timing to perform all of the swinging and circling movements which make up asymmetric bar work.

Floor and Vault

The other two women's exercises are vault and floor. The vault calls for speed and agility. The floor exercises are done to music and contain the widest range of movements in gymnastics. During her routine, the gymnast tries to show her agility, suppleness and acrobatic skill.

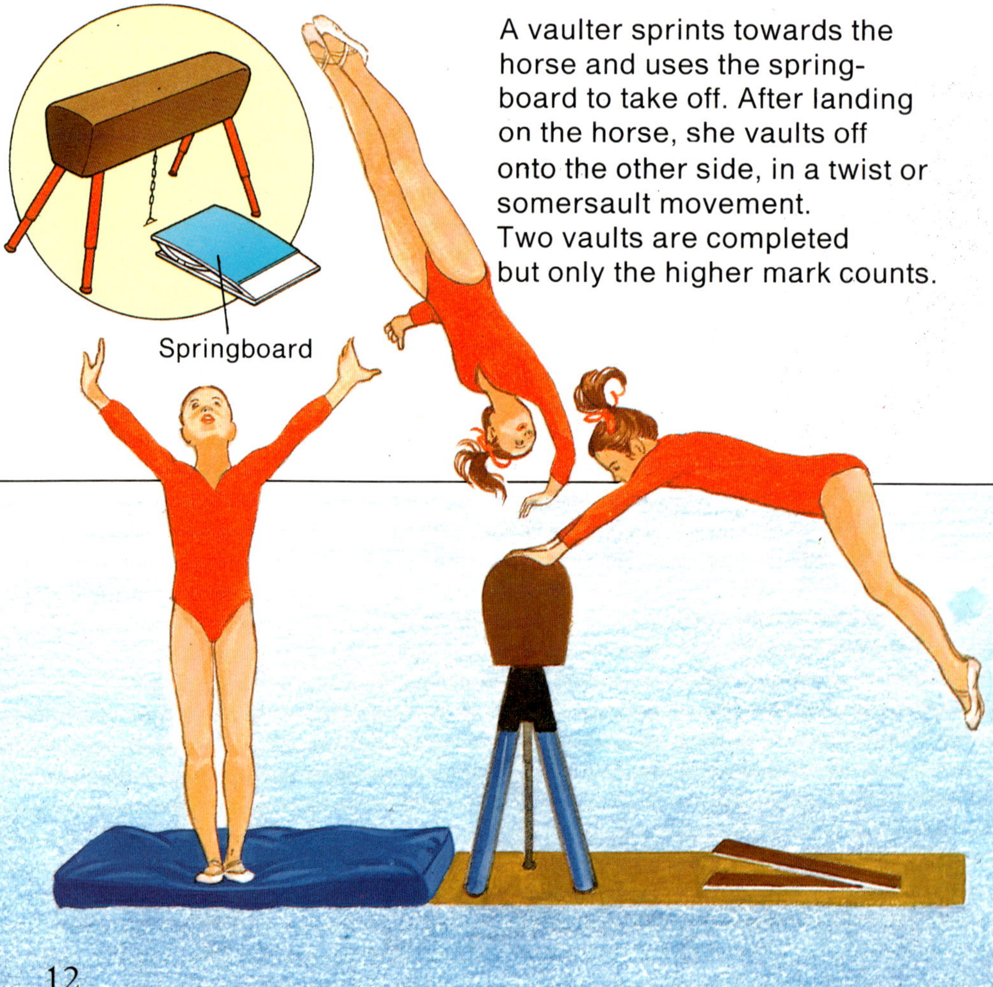

A vaulter sprints towards the horse and uses the spring-board to take off. After landing on the horse, she vaults off onto the other side, in a twist or somersault movement. Two vaults are completed but only the higher mark counts.

FLOOR EXERCISE

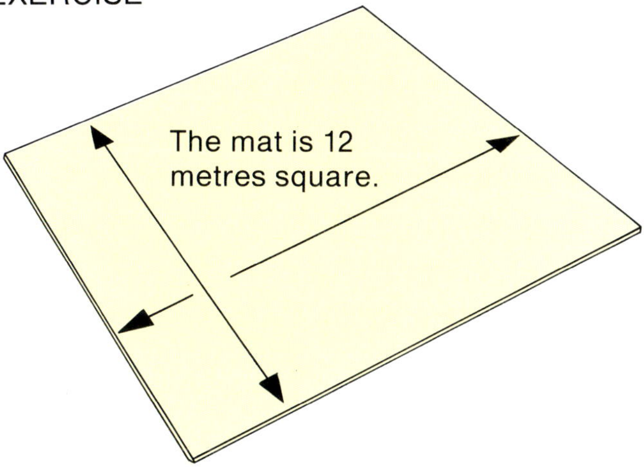

The floor exercise has to contain three tumble runs which are made from corner to corner. The rest of the routine is made up of turns, balances, jumps and leaps, linked together with dance movements. The gymnast should use the whole area of the mat.

Bars and Pommel Horse

Male artistic gymnasts perform on six pieces of apparatus. They need great strength and excellent timing to make the swinging movements that are needed for exercises on the horizontal bar, the parallel bars and the pommel horse.

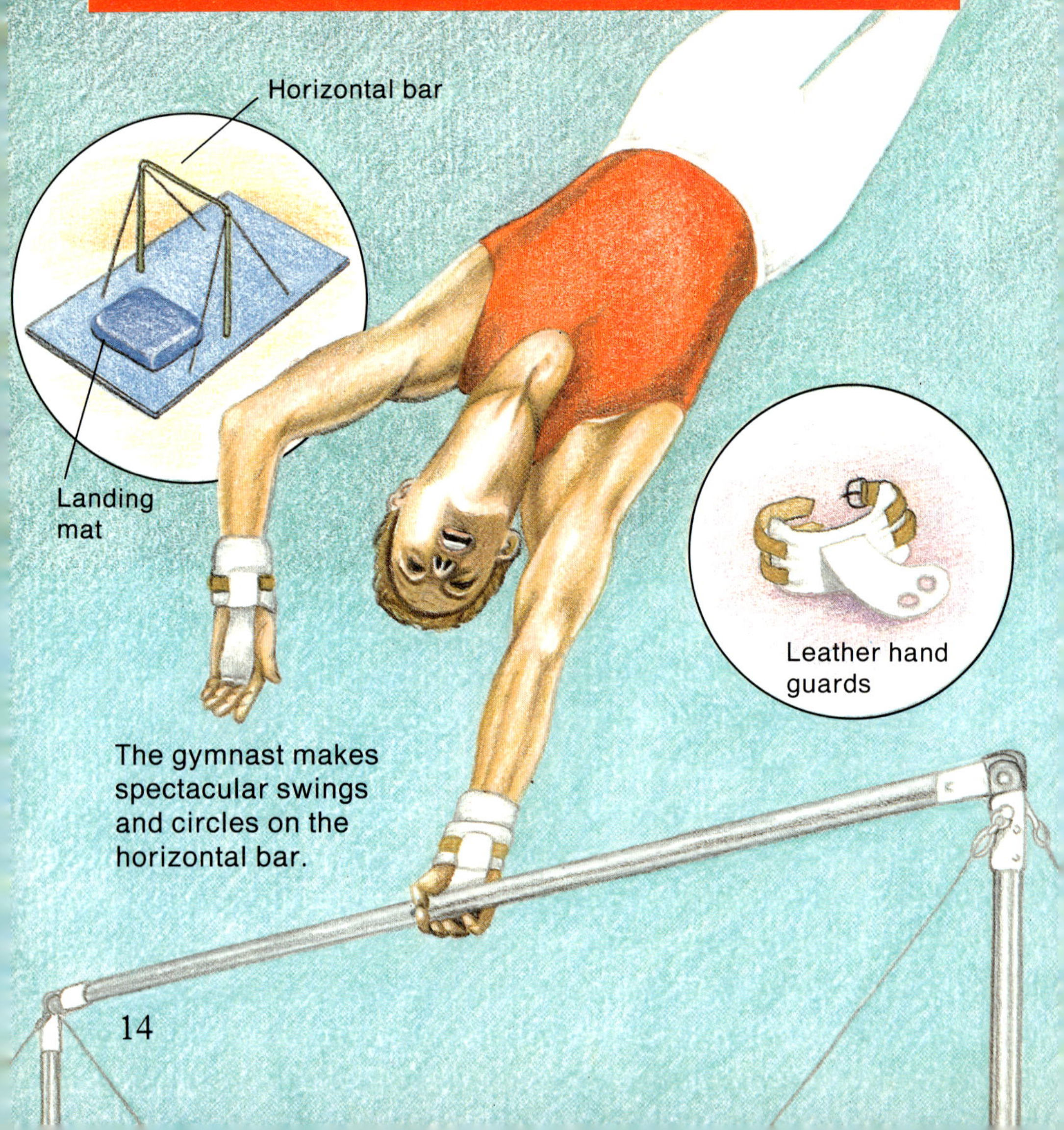

The gymnast makes spectacular swings and circles on the horizontal bar.

PARALLEL BARS

The men's parallel bars are at equal heights.

Balances have to be held for at least two seconds.

Gymnasts pause between swings to hold balances.

Strength and balance are tested on the pommel horse.

Rings, Floor and Vault

The other three pieces of apparatus used by men are the rings, the floor mat and the vaulting horse. The floor exercise is shorter than the women's, and the men show off their agility, strength and balance rather than their grace and suppleness.

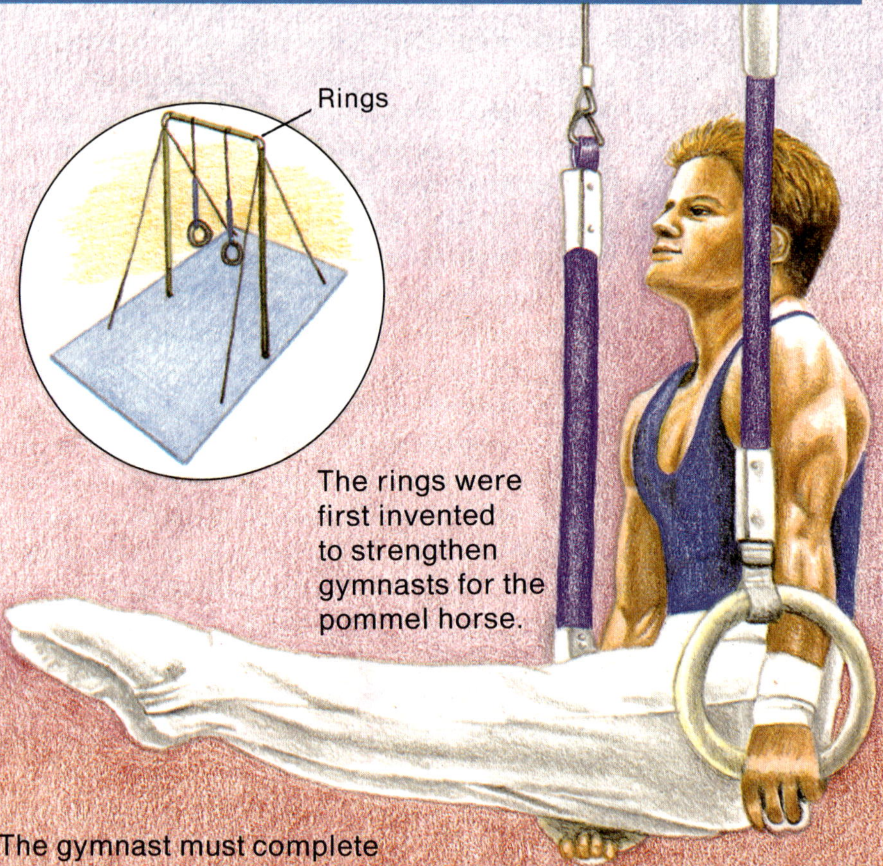

The rings were first invented to strengthen gymnasts for the pommel horse.

The gymnast must complete his routine without swinging the rings. This needs enormous strength.

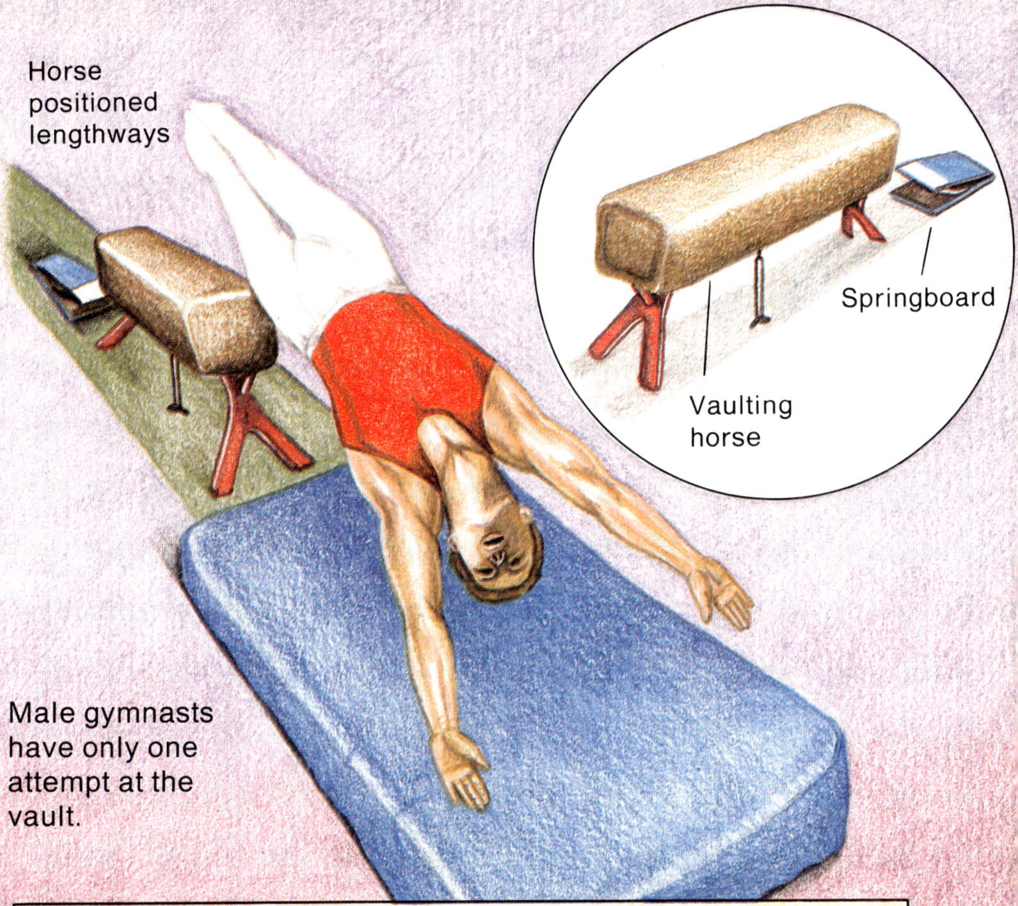

Male gymnasts have only one attempt at the vault.

FLOOR EXERCISE

Routines are made up of tumbles and balances.

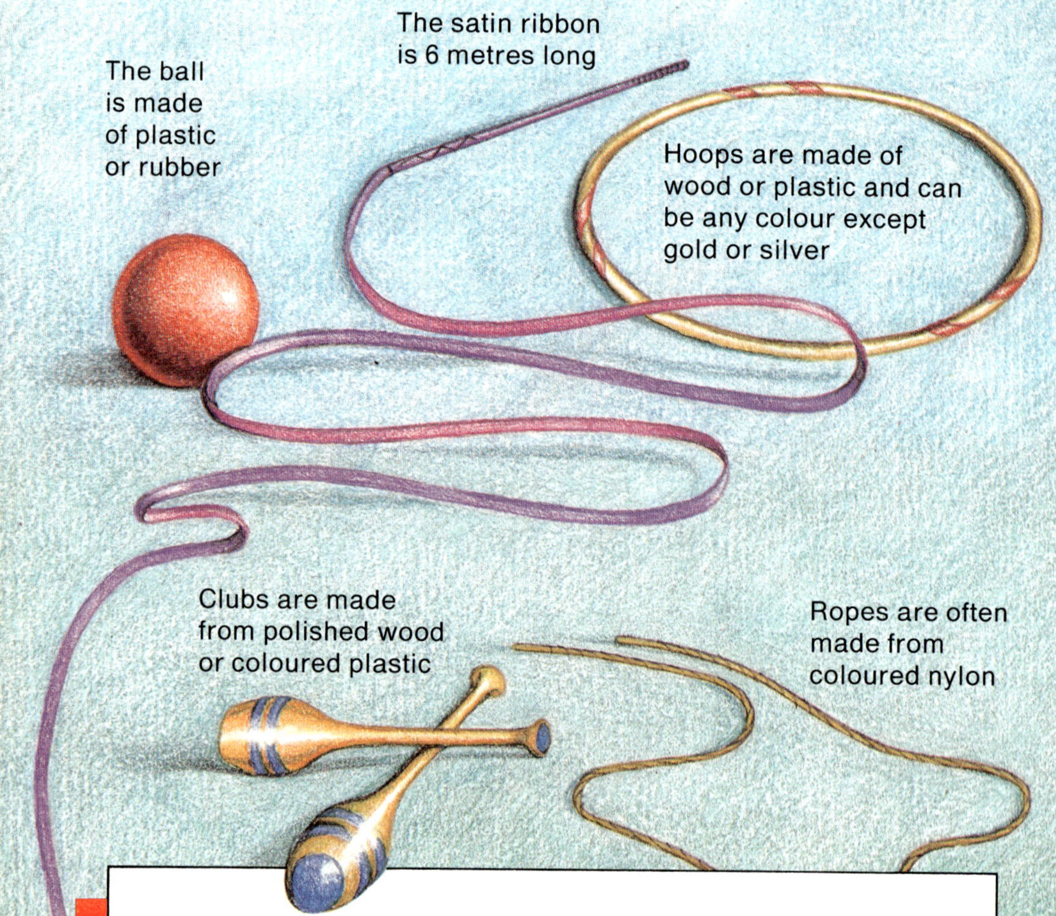

Rhythmic Gymnastics

Rhythmic gymnastics is for women only. They perform on the mat with one of the five pieces of hand apparatus shown above. The gymnasts use dancing, gymnastics and juggling skills all at the same time. They do their routines to music, and have to keep the apparatus moving all the time.

◀ The ball is thrown in the air, or bounced. It cannot be held, but has to be balanced on the palm of the hand.

▶ The gymnast can skip or jump through the rope. It can also be thrown in the air.

▲ The two clubs are swung, twirled and thrown in the air. They can even be bounced or rolled on the floor.

▶ The hoop can be thrown in the air, bounced or rolled along.

Team Events

Rhythmic gymnastics can also be performed by teams of up to six women gymnasts. In team events the gymnasts can use more than one type of apparatus. The gymnasts perform with their own apparatus, but must also exchange them with other members of the team at least four times.

The twirling patterns of the ribbon create some of the most beautiful effects in rhythmic gymnastics.

TEAM ROUTINES

Team routines last longer than individual routines, and a team of six gymnasts will perform for up to three minutes. Each exchange of apparatus must be done in a different way. During the routine, the team must make at least six different formations on the floor. The judges award marks for individual skills, for the harmony of the group work, and for the quality and originality of the choreography.

◀ A mixed pair. There are also men's and women's pairs.

▶ One section of the men's fours exercise is the set pyramid. Only one gymnast may have his feet on the ground.

Sports Acrobatics

Sports acrobatics are rather like circus performances. Solo gymnasts perform tumble runs which include double and even triple backward somersaults. Team events involve making pyramids to show the gymnasts' strength and balance, and tempo routines, in which one of the gymnasts is thrown by the other members of the team.

During the tempo, throws and somersaults are performed to music.

Routines last about three minutes.

IMPORTANT
You must never try any of these tricks or tumbles without proper safety mats or supervision by a qualified coach.

Preparing Yourself

Gymnasts need to keep their bodies in top physical shape. This is not simply a matter of doing a few exercises – diet and sleeping habits are also very important. Gymnasts should also wear neat clothing which will not interfere with their performance.

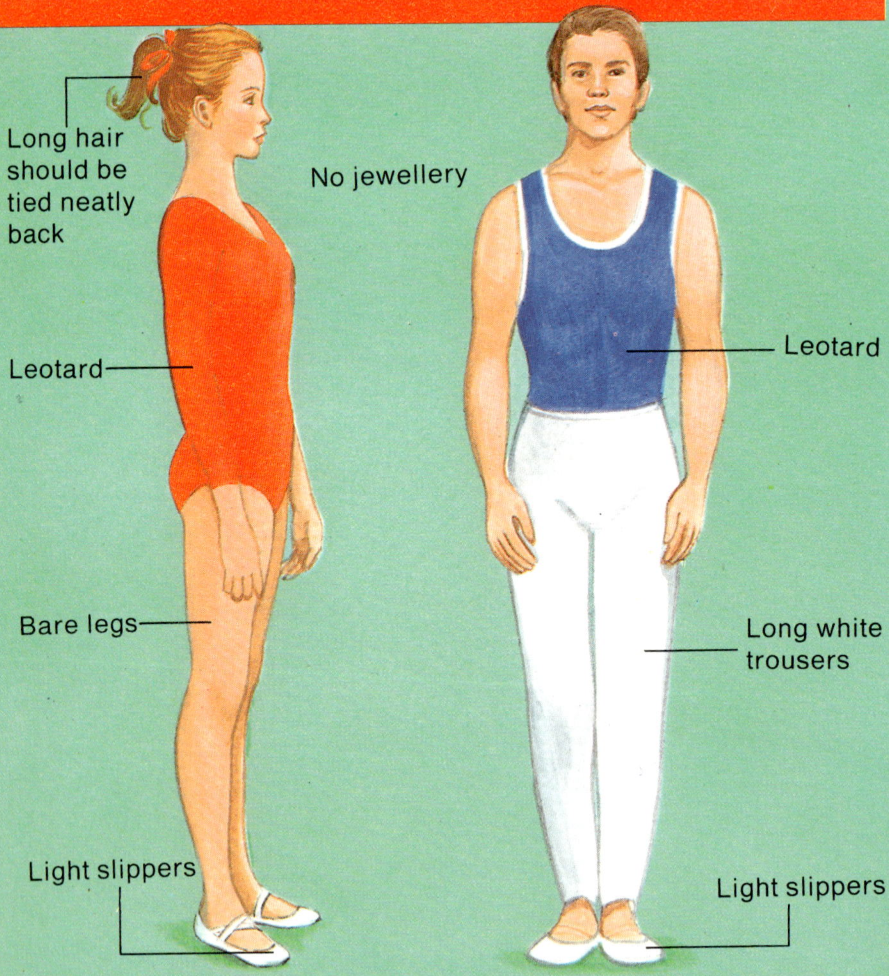

◀ Cut out any unhealthy eating habits. Gymnasts avoid eating too much fatty or sweet food.

► A sensible diet with plenty of salad, fruit and fish helps to keep gymnasts slim and fit.

WARMING UP

Warming up prevents muscle strains and tears. Try to do these simple exercises thoroughly, rather than quickly.

Gentle head rolling

Arm circling

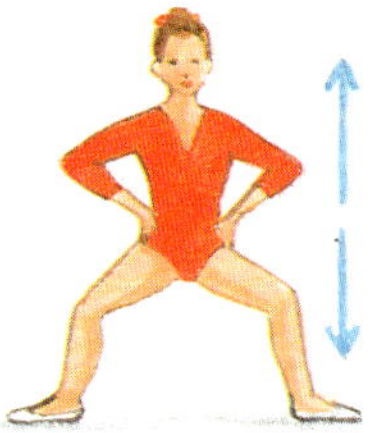

Bending and stretching knees

Circling the ankles

Jumping on the spot

Twisting upper body

Bending upper body

Touching your toes

Be Supple – Be Strong

A gymnast needs the strength of a weight-lifter, the suppleness of a ballet dancer and the agility of a trapeze artist. Unfortunately these skills do not come naturally, so all gymnasts need to work hard to keep their bodies in good condition. Jogging is good for all-round fitness, but special exercises are needed to develop strength and suppleness.

1

1. Sit with the soles of your feet pressed together. Press your knees down gently towards the floor.

2

2. Bend your front leg and lean your weight on to it, like a fencer lunging forward.

3

3. Start in a crouch. Keep your hands pressed flat on the floor and try to straighten your legs.

4

4. Try to push your shoulders down as far as possible in this position.

5

5. Keeping your back straight and toes pointed, reach along your left leg as far as you can. Repeat with your right leg.

6. Squat down, then straighten your legs to jump as high as possible. Repeat.

7. Lie on your back with your legs bent. Put your arms behind your head and sit up slowly.

8. Lie on your tummy. Lift your head and legs at the same time to arch your back as much as possible.

9. Lean against a wall and push off from it as if you were doing press-ups.

Unless you land with bent legs and straight back, you could damage your spine.

All stretching should be done slowly and gently. Make sure you avoid these two common mistakes.

In a crab, keep shoulders and knees bent to protect your spine.

Your Own Routine

You can have fun making up your own routine. You should only do this in a gym, with a properly qualified instructor to help you. Choose a piece of music which lasts between 45 seconds and one minute. Practise arm gestures, dance steps and attractive poses in the mirror. Plan your route around the floor, using as much space as possible.

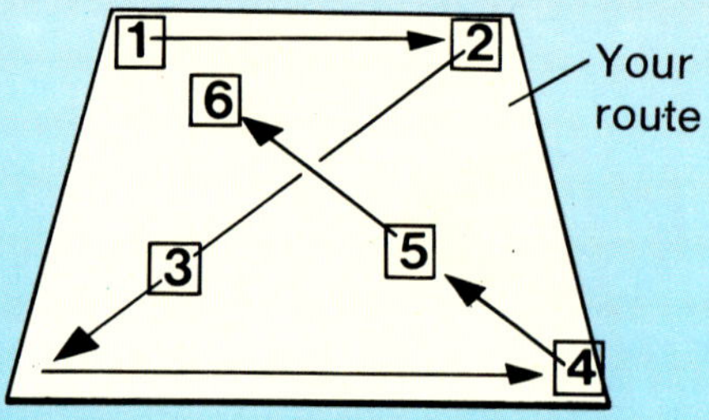

1. Keep your body straight and make a full-turn jump. Bend the knees to cushion the landing.

2. Try to form a shape like this, with a straight supporting leg.

3. Do a cartwheel, making a good star shape.

4. Do a forward roll, keeping your back rounded. Push against the floor with your hands at the start to cushion the impact.

5. Do a straight upward jump with a half turn, then sit back and roll back to a shoulder stand. Use your hands to hold your hips high, as here.

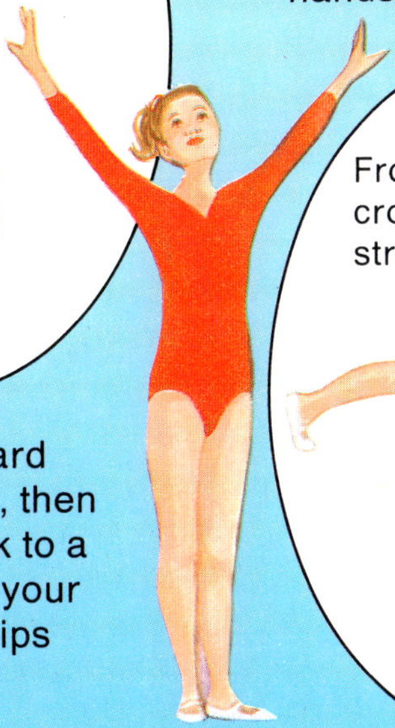

6. Push up from a lying position. Jump so that your feet are just behind your hands, then straighten up.

Glossary

Acrobat
An entertainer who performs gymnastic feats, such as tumbles and balances.

Agility
The skill of moving the body, arms and feet quickly and neatly.

Apparatus
A piece of equipment used in gymnastics. Those used in artistic gymnastics, such as the horizontal bar or vaulting horse, are large and stand on the floor. The apparatus used in rhythmic gymnastics is much smaller and can be held in the hand.

Arabesque
A balance on one foot, with the other foot lifted high at the back while the body is tilted forward.

Artistic gymnastics
The main type of gymnastics, where gymnasts perform on a floor mat or on different pieces of apparatus such as the beam or rings.

Asymmetric bars
A piece of apparatus used by women. It consists of two horizontal bars, one higher than the other.

Choreography
The dance steps which are put into a gymnastic routine.

Exercise
A single movement in gymnastics.

Gymnasium
A building used for gymnastics.

Hand guard
A leather hand protector.

Horizontal bar
A high bar used in men's artistic gymnastics.

Leotard
A tight-fitting costume.

Parallel bars
A piece of apparatus used in artistic gymnastics consisting of two parallel bars set at equal heights.

Podium
A raised platform on which gymnastics events are held.

Pommel horse
A piece of apparatus used in men's artistic gymnastics.

Pyramid
A human tower made during sports acrobatics.

Rhythmic gymnastics
A branch of gymnastics in which women and girls use hand-held apparatus.

Routine
A series of exercises joined together into a single sequence to make a display.

Shoulder stand
A balance in gymnastics where the body is supported on the shoulders.

Sports acrobatics
A branch of gymnastics in which gymnasts perform acrobatics alone or in groups.

Suppleness
A wide range of movement in the joints of the body.

Tempo
Part of a routine in sports acrobatics when one of the gymnasts is thrown by the others.

Trapeze artist
A circus performer who does tricks on high swings.

Tumblers
Originally medieval acrobats and travelling performers. Now taken to mean anyone who performs acrobatics.

Tumble run
A run, often diagonally across the mat, during which a gymnast performs a series of tumbles joined together into a single routine.

Tumbling
A solo event in sports acrobatics. It includes flips, springs and somersaults. Tumbling is also part of the floor exercises in artistic gymnastics.

Vaulting horse
A leather-covered box on legs, over which gymnasts jump using a springboard to help them take off.

Index